C000178256

THE BOOKKEEPER
RISES

BUILD A SUCCESSFUL BOOKKEEPING BUSINESS
THAT WORKS FOR YOU AND GIVES YOU THE
LIFE YOU REALLY WANT

Jo Wood and Zoe Whitman

PRAISE FOR
THE BOOKKEEPER RISES

66 *Everything I wish I'd known before starting my bookkeeping practice, and more*

- Kathryn Frimond, Your Local Bookkeeper

66 *A must have read for anyone who is thinking about, or already has a bookkeeping business. In just a few hours you will know almost everything there is to know, and learn from the experiences of others. The honesty and openness in this book reflects the 6FB group in real life and that's the best way for us to learn. Honest, open, empathetic, guiding and supportive. Just amazing.*

- Claire Johnson, Bluebell Admin Services

66 *Our time is precious and should be spent doing the things that bring us the most joy so take full advantage of Jo and Zoe sharing their learnings rather than reinventing the wheel and spending months (if not years!) researching everything for yourself. Wherever you are in your bookkeeping or accountancy practice journey, this book will leave you inspired, motivated and empowered to create the future you and your loved ones deserve.*

- Laura Day-Henderson, More than Bookkeeping

66 *What a great introduction and insight into the world of running a bookkeeping business! Jo and Zoe guide you through each section, holding your hand the entire way, in what feels like a chat amongst old friends. A definite read for all those aspiring to run their own practice!*

- Clare Martin

66 *Jo and Zoe have taken the bookkeeping world by storm! The love and drive they have for the bookkeeping industry is shown by their determination and knowledge to make us be seen, heard, and valued in the wider community. This is a book not to be left on the shelf if you are thinking of making that leap. I wish they were around when I started my business.*

- Donna Haslewood, Artisan Accountant & Co

66 *As someone about to establish my own practice, this book has been highly valuable and incredibly well timed. Jo and Zoe share their bookkeeping business tips and experiences in a way which is engaging, supportive and informative. This book will inspire you to reflect on the current position of your business and to start implementing improvements.*

- Rebecca Holmes

66 *I wish I had read this book when I first started my practice and saved myself lots of time and heartache! Everything you need to know, from practical tips to mindset, is in here.*

- Carly Clark, Conqueror Accountancy

66 *This book is a great read, it doesn't matter if you have not started your business or been running it for many years like me. The book will offer you a chance to revisit your business and review what you are doing and how you can improve efficiencies and give you a great springboard to building the business you want to that allows you to build the life that you want. Add the book to the online support group, and you have one of the best resources for any bookkeeping business starting or well established. The group helped me turn my business around, and will help you not fall into the same traps.*

- Leanda Daddow, Celtic Bookkeeping

For our ever supportive husbands, Paul and Olly.

And for our children, Daniel, Grace, Rosie, Heidi and Wilf who give us reason to strive every day.

Contents

PART 2: INSPIRATIONAL STORIES – 161

Foreword

by James Ashford

My first business failed.

It didn't fail for any major reason, but because of a series of seemingly small decisions I made, all connected to the finance function of that business, or rather lack thereof.

I was making decisions based on outdated and inaccurate financial information, without a clear plan and no clue whether I was on track or not.

The pain of that failure was huge.

It led to us remortgaging our house, my marriage breaking down and me having to rebuild everything from the ground up.

When I started in business again, I swore I would invest heavily into its finance function.

I wanted clear financial goals, a budget, a cashflow forecast, monthly management accounts so I knew I was on track, total visibility of everything that was going on with updated, accurate information.

I also didn't want any of it to take any of my time or my team's time, so we could all focus on our highest value activities in driving the business forward.

At the heart of that business was excellent financial data collection (bookkeeping).

None of the systems could function if we weren't getting accurate financial data in, on a daily and weekly basis.

This was all underpinned by impeccable bookkeeping.

To my mind, bookkeeping is the key to the city of gold.

Without it, everything crumbles.

With it, I can make strategic decisions about the direction and growth of my business, whilst focussing on my highest value activities within my business or my family, friends, health and wealth outside of my business.

That's what great bookkeeping enables.

You are not just a bookkeeper… you have the power to unlock everything an entrepreneur is looking to achieve.

With this finance function in place, I was able to build and scale a very successful and profitable business called GoProposal, to £1.5m in revenue, which I then sold to Sage PLC. And let me tell you, when you have a PLC carrying out due diligence on your business, bringing in a top four accounting business to review everything since day dot, you better hope and pray that EVERYTHING is impeccable… and it was.

Just before we sold, we were investing about £6,000 a month into our finance function, of which £3,500 went towards bookkeeping.

Because of the quality of our record keeping and the transparency it enabled, we were able to command a high fee for the business.

So I LOVE bookkeepers, because of everything they've allowed me to create in my life.

But building a successful bookkeeping practice is tough... especially in these challenging and turbulent times.

You are great at your craft, but you don't know what you don't know and when you start your bookkeeping business, you don't just get given all of the skills you need around pricing, selling, marketing, recruitment, managing staff, systemising, what tech to use, the list goes on... and it's overwhelming.

On top of that, it's lonely.

So you don't end up with a bookkeeping business, you end up with a job, and it's a crap job, because there's a lot of pressure, it's low paid, you can't go on holiday, you can never be sick, and it's tiring... UNLESS... unless you're shown how to build a highly successful bookkeeping business.

But to achieve that, you need people who have done it, been there and more importantly, know how to help you to get there too.

For many years now I have been a huge fan of Jo and Zoe.

I love their passion and enthusiasm for the industry, their depth of experience and their ability to impart that hard earned knowledge through their 5-step Framework.

They are massively shortcutting the growth of bookkeepers and accelerating their growth with proven, tried and tested systems, strategies and a winning mindset.

They build the support structure around you that you desperately need, throwing a hand down to help you up the hard parts and inviting you to help and inspire others too.

This book is filled with accelerating strategies, those winning mindsets and inspirational stories to drive you forward and upwards.

You are not just a bookkeeper.

You have the power to transform business and people's lives.

And I should know, because people like you transformed mine.

I want you to win. I want you to succeed... I NEED you to.

And with this book, together with Jo and Zoe's support... you will.

James Ashford

Founder of GoProposal

Introduction

Have you ever felt that you are meant for something bigger – something better?

I have had this gut feeling for years. I even had it as a child. I just knew that I was meant for greatness.

This could come across as arrogant, but I promise you it's not. I have always wanted to help others succeed, and being a big sister to four younger siblings meant there was always someone that needed help. I started tutoring children in Maths and English when I was only 15, and even though that helped me decide that a career in teaching children was not what I wanted to do long-term, I did love the feeling of sharing my wisdom and seeing my students' eyes light up when they finally understood something that had previously puzzled them.

When I left school and joined an accountancy firm as an apprentice, it was me that needed help. I remember looking at my bank statements and being utterly confused as to why the debits and credits at work were the other way round!

That all seems a very long time ago. Over the years, as I learned and studied more, I yet again became the tutor. To colleagues, to business owners and to family members, I had built up a steady knowledge of both bookkeeping and business. People liked to pick my brains.

In 2018 this gut instinct reared its head again. My father had passed away the year before, at just 57, and this really made me realise how precious life is and how I must fulfil any deep desires.

On 12th February 2018, on the anniversary of my dad's passing, I signed up to a coaching programme with a lady I had been following intently for many years. Her programme was going to cost me £10,000 and even though I believed I couldn't afford it, I also believed I couldn't afford not to do it.

The course was designed to help you find out what your passion was and how you could make a living by turning this idea into an online business. I had no idea what this would be, and this was also scary because I feared I would never figure it out.

I did figure it out, though, and here we are today. Working with a coach, a structured programme and a cohort of fabulous entrepreneurs, I found how I could build a business that was aligned with my passion. From there, the 6 Figure Bookkeepers' Club was born.

At this time I was working in industry full-time for one business as a finance director. I loved the work, the team and everything about the business, but I knew that serving only one business was playing small. I knew that what I was doing for this one business was what every small- to medium-sized business needed. I was offering clear, accurate bookkeeping, monthly management accounts, and improvements across all systems. I was also a sounding board for senior management to air future plans with. I got to thinking: why are only big businesses allowed access to this type of service? Small business owners need this – in some cases more than larger companies with in-house accounts departments. In the past I had offered an outsourced accounts department service, but never a virtual finance director service. I knew this could be amazing, but it was still too small. I could only serve so many clients – even if I took on lots of staff it wouldn't impact the millions of small businesses that needed this service. I needed to share what I knew with all the bookkeepers out there, so I set up the 6 Figure Bookkeepers' Club Facebook group and went to work on writing the course.

I was still working full-time at that point, and I was feeling a bit of a fraud as I wasn't running my own firm at the time. Well, as they say, be careful what you wish for. I was made redundant from my perfect job in April 2019. I still to this day have no idea why, but I like to believe that the universe had different plans for me.

So here I was in the position of starting up a brand new practice from scratch. Due to previous contracts and non-compete clauses, I could not approach any of my previous clients from earlier practices. This presented me with an amazing opportunity. I could use my course outline as a guide while adding everything I had omitted as I went through the motions. In my first year, my turnover reached £67k and in year two I was on track to hit £145k, and after six months we incorporated. In my first year as a limited company we hit £210k and this year we are working towards £300k

In November 2019 I was asked by the Institute of Certified Bookkeepers (ICB) to be a keynote speaker at their annual Bookkeepers Summit. I was nervous, but as my mindset and personal development had taught me, pushing through comfort zones is imperative if you hope to grow. I said yes.

I was very pleased to see that one of the other keynotes was Zoe Whitman. I had been part of a meeting with Zoe and the ICB when we reviewed the new management accounts syllabus with them. Zoe had a small baby so had attended the meeting via Zoom, and we had also bumped into each other at Xerocon earlier that month.

I knew that Zoe was my sort of person – just much cooler than me in her pumps and dress – I could never pull that off. I remember that I briefly spoke to her regarding the idea I had. I knew she had a similar passion to me or else she wouldn't be preparing to speak on stage in front of hundreds of bookkeepers. We decided that we would connect and catch up over the phone in the following weeks. We did that, and I shared more about the course and my vision. She was 100% behind the idea and we had a feeling that doing this together would benefit us both. I was now super busy trying to build a business, be a mum to my three, and stay sane.

We decided that we couldn't start a business without getting to know each other properly, and that needed to be in person. Being on opposite sides of the country meant we were going to have to meet in the middle. We both looked at a map and decided on Reading.

I booked a two-bed apartment on the river and we met there one cold but bright-skied weekend in January 2020. Luckily we got on straight away and quickly got to work mapping out how this business could work. The floor was covered in wrapping paper, which was used as a base for the hundreds of post-it notes that we quickly scribbled on as we brainstormed our ideas. It became clear very quickly that we really liked each other and that we could build a business that would help to solve hundreds of bookkeepers' and business owners' problems. We knew that although people looking to train as a bookkeeper had their pick of training providers and colleges, once they had qualified there was no quality business advice or coaching on how to start and grow a successful and profitable bookkeeping practice.

By Sunday afternoon we had incorporated the company, set up the website and expanded the course outline to include every title of every lesson.

We were in business and we knew that we could make this work virtually across the country – and thank goodness we could. In February 2020 I made my first ever journey to Bristol to stay with Zoe and her family. Zoe had arranged a photoshoot and a meeting with a software company to discuss our plans. This was the last time I saw Zoe before the Covid-19 lockdowns. Again, I feel that we were so lucky to have had that time to get our photos taken and that I was able to spend some quality time with her family.

Nowadays, Zoe and I speak to each other daily over voice notes on Whatsapp, as well as via weekly Zoom calls and our podcasts.

As I write, The 6 Figure Bookkeepers' Club, our community on Facebook, has hit 7,000 members. We also have over 100 members on one of our many courses.

This is just the start of our journey and we are so pleased that you are here with us and we both wish you and your practice every success for the future.

Jo Wood, April '22

Part 1

How to Launch and Grow your Bookkeeping Business

RESET

We go searching for the how, but what we don't do is understand who we need to become.

~ Baiju Solanki

Chapter 1

GETTING STARTED

The essentials

There's a lot to do before you take on your first bookkeeping client. You're starting a business and you have responsibilities to run your business properly and look after your clients. At the same time, you're entering a profession that requires you to handle data and financial information, so there are certain legal and regulatory requirements with which you have to comply. This can feel daunting and overwhelming, and that overwhelm can be the reason that many bookkeepers simply don't get their practices started.

You picked up this book because you want to start a bookkeeping practice, so maybe you've felt this overwhelm too. And we're going to start with a simple suggestion.

If you're feeling unable to get started, we recommend you make a list of what you need to do – a simple list. And know that you don't have to do every single thing right now.

There's no hurry.

Take your time.

There are many, many things which will be added to that list as you go on this journey.

Get it right and feel good about it. Then you'll be able to move forward with confidence.

We recommend that you book an hour or two in your diary every week for the next month and work through the things on your list one at a time.

In fact, when you've finished with that list, once you've finished the box ticking and what we think of as the "start-up admin", you can keep that recurring appointment with yourself to carry on working on your business, so you're in the best place to grow and so that your business doesn't grow without you making any decisions about how that's going to happen.

So, back to starting up.

The very first thing to think about is your professional training. Depending on whether you are new to the bookkeeping profession or a seasoned finance professional, you may already be a member of a professional body, or you might want to join one and complete some training to make sure you have the knowledge and skills you need before you take on your first client.

As a bookkeeper or finance professional, we expect you're highly versed with the different business structures. And before you start to think about the businesses of any clients, it's important to get clear on the structure of your own.

Jo: In April 2019 I was made redundant from a job I loved.

The role had started out as a lead from an accountant I had been working with two and a half years previously. The accountant had said that they needed two days of help getting their bank reconciliations up to date, but after less than an hour onsite, I knew that the company needed so much more than that.

I could see great potential, but there were no standard processes and they had no idea where their business stood from a financial perspective. I needed more work at the time so I wrote the managing director a proposal setting out how I could help the business improve and become more profitable. They took me on part-time initially and then over time I became their full time finance manager.

I thoroughly enjoyed implementing processes that impacted the bottom line, and my work was having a direct impact on the bank account. Over the next two years the net profit went from £0 to £1,000,000 (combined net profit for two years). I loved my job and the amazing team, and I felt at the top of my game.

Unfortunately, for reasons unknown to me, I was suddenly made redundant. That time presented the hardest but best struggle I've ever had to experience.

I had no choice but to replace my income by building a successful bookkeeping business from scratch. If I had not had this experience I would not be here with Zoe sharing and passing on what I learnt from that period in my life.

Did I do everything perfectly? No!

Did I cry and doubt myself? Yes!

Have I grown as a person and a business owner because of this? Absolutely!!

One of my biggest mistakes was that I set up as a sole trader. Even though my goal (and absolute must) was to earn the £70k per year I'd lost from my employment, I didn't believe that I was worthy or capable of growing a business big enough to warrant limited company status. In hindsight I think this was because I was feeling extremely fragile and vulnerable, so imposter syndrome was kicking in big time.

What this led to was me having to turn my sole trader practice into a limited company 18 months after setting up. This caused me so much extra admin and headaches. I find it quite funny that I couldn't see what I was capable of, but I'm annoyed at myself at the same time.

Our advice is to set up the business you want to run in the future from the start. This means giving some deep thought to your goals, which we appreciate can be difficult at the start of a business. If you've never done this before, you might doubt yourself. You might have imposter syndrome – you might never expect that you'll actually be able to make this your full-time business because of an excuse you're telling yourself or something that's holding you back from your past. It could be a belief that you're not good enough or an expectation that you'll fail.

We work with successful bookkeepers every day who are building amazing businesses which support their families, which have reached six figures in turnover and beyond, who now employ teams, who have the freedom to work only school hours if they wish to. We know you can make this business a success if you get the support you need and dare to believe in yourself.

Throughout the rest of the book, we're going to take you through a framework we teach bookkeepers who join some of our virtual events. It takes you through what you need to do to find clients and build a successful business.

Finding clients is essential for your success, but so that you don't set about building a business which is unprofitable, inflexible and makes you unhappy, we want to talk to you about the very first step of the framework right now. The first step is to reset.

Reset everything you believe about your abilities to start and grow this business, every limiting belief. This is the time to decide what you want, to set goals and make plans. We want you to consider what you want your business to be doing in the future, because that will give you the best chance of succeeding in the future.

So let's go back to your business structure. What will be right for the business you want to run in the future which allows you to achieve your goals in business and in life? Do you want to work as a sole trader or will a limited company structure serve you better?

Depending on your goals for your business, your financial situation, and factors such as whether you're planning to work as a sole practitioner or with a business partner or to employ staff, you can choose to set up your business as a sole trader, a partnership or a limited company.

Each of these comes with its own merits from risk, liability and taxation perspectives, and only you will know what is best for you. Jo's lesson highlights that getting this right on day one will save you work if you outgrow your business structure, so take some time now to give this the thought it needs.

Like Jo, you can change things if at a later date you find that your setup isn't working for you, so don't let the detail be an excuse for inaction if you're feeling stuck. Just be mindful that making a choice aligned with your long-term goals now might save you some time in the future.

Once you know through which legal structure you will trade, you will most likely then apply for a practising certificate with a professional body. Most of the bookkeepers we work with choose to do this. It gives them the support of a professional organisation, as well as credibility. The application process can take time, so start this process early and get other foundations in place while you wait.

In the UK, training on the anti money laundering regulations is crucial. As bookkeepers, dealing with bank statements and seeing intimate information about our clients' affairs, we are the first line of defence for detecting fraud and illegal activity. For the purposes of complying with anti money laundering regulations and legislation, one of the things you must decide on is who will supervise your practice for your Anti Money Laundering duties. Your professional body will most likely support you with this, and you can also look at HMRC's website for current guidance on their requirements as well as for approved training.

Decide who will supervise your practice and then make sure you know what you need to do to comply with their requirements. Find out how you would go about reporting anything suspicious, and determine how you will build this critical work into your processes.

You will also need to consider insurances. As a bookkeeper you need to hold professional indemnity insurance in case a claim is made against you as a professional, and you might also need public liability insurance, employers' insurance, or contents insurance for your equipment and client records depending on where and how you work and whether you employ a team.

As a handler and processor of data, you will need to register with the body responsible for data in your country. In the UK this is the Information Commissioner's Office, and there are various policies your practice will need to have informing clients, potential clients and website visitors of how you use their data when they work with you or contact you.

With these foundations in place, you'll be ready to start thinking about some of the more exciting elements of running your own business.

See your business as a business

Every business needs a highly skilled bookkeeper to look after the accounts. Luckily, you are a highly skilled bookkeeper. But one of the traps we see bookkeepers in our community falling into is failing to see themselves as a business owner.

You have your business structure sorted and you've done what is necessary to set up a business that can offer a bookkeeping service. Now it's time to think about that service, and the first step we all must take is to shake off the idea of being just a bookkeeper.

We talk about mindset a lot with our community of bookkeepers. Your belief in yourself and your business is crucial for building your success. In fact, we think it's so important that a whole module of our Bookkeepers' 6 Month Success Programme is all about mindset. Mindset is part of the 5-step Framework we teach. We weave it through absolutely everything we do. So before we go any further, repeat after us:

"I am the CEO of my business."

> You are not just a bookkeeper. You are now a business owner. Just like all of your future clients, you are building a business and you are in charge of your business's success.

Why is this so important?

Because bookkeepers who fail to see that they run a business end up transacting one hour of bookkeeping for one hour of payment. And it feels great when you start out. Maybe you've worked in a bookkeeping or finance-related role in the past. And maybe you've been paid £10 or £15 or even £20 per hour to do that. When you started your business, you probably thought about what you'd charge and decided to double your hourly rate. You thought that even after a bit of tax, you'd be way better off.

But what you didn't think about was the holiday you might like to take next summer, the times your child would be off school sick, how you'd pay for some software you'd want to invest in to make you more efficient in your work, or the fact that the growth of your business would be limited by the hours you have available in the day. Failure to acknowledge the final point here is the reason so many bookkeepers who start a business to have flexibility around their children fail to ever get that flexibility. They want to earn more but their business hasn't been set up to allow them to do that.

> We must move on from the belief that we simply deliver a service in exchange for hourly payment.

Right now, while your business is made up of just you (or maybe just you plus a friend or family member), you are in control of every aspect of your business. No matter how simple you want to keep your business (and we promise that it can be simple if you want it to be), your role needs to be so much more than finding clients and doing their bookkeeping. As the owner of a successful business, you need to take control of everything – from customer services to operations to HR to marketing. And we say take control so that we don't leave it to chance – or our clients – to determine what our business looks like.

You can build a business that works for you. But you have to design it.

If that seems like quite a lot when you're just looking for your first couple of clients, consider this.

It goes without saying that the bookkeeping you do must be up to scratch. As professionals, we have a reputation to uphold, and you've probably decided to start this business because you are a good bookkeeper.

Many bookkeepers who go into business get stuck here, though. They ensure the bank account is always reconciled and that filings are done on time. They chase up debtors – they really provide a brilliant service. Unsure how to go about pricing for what they do, they charge their client an hourly rate, but that hourly rate results in them remaining effectively an employee with many bosses. They have no time to find new clients and no way to ever bring support into their businesses. This leaves our bookkeepers overworked and tired, saying no to new clients as they're at capacity with no idea of how to scale.

Doing great bookkeeping is great for your reputation as a bookkeeper. We know you do a great job. But when we keep small, our businesses are only about us. We know that if you don't step back and work on your business, your business won't be able to grow and won't be as profitable as you'd like it to be.

We don't think you started your business so you could work weekends and evenings when you get busy. We don't think you started out so that you could work for a lower fee than you would in a job just to get a few clients.

And if you don't work on your business now, we know that you are unlikely to build the business that you want to run. We've seen it many times. We don't want you to feel you'd be better off in the job that you were hoping to escape by becoming self-employed, so let's think bigger.

Think bigger

Think of a large business.

Who did you think of?

Maybe you thought of Amazon, EasyJet or HSBC. You might have thought of The Body Shop, Ikea, or Manchester United. Whichever brand came to mind, we expect you thought of a huge organisation. And those businesses have managers, internal systems, sales departments, and worldwide teams. But one day they started off as just an idea. They started off as small businesses, just like your bookkeeping practice will, but in order to be ready to scale and grow, they had to be designed and created with the infrastructure that would get them to where they wanted to be. We're not suggesting that you intend to grow to the size of Amazon, but being aware that your small (for now) business needs to consider the departments it will need to scale will help you move to the mindset you need for success.

Take a step back and imagine yourself in your office, running your bookkeeping business in the future. You are the CEO. You have hundreds of clients as well as staff and premises. This doesn't have to be your vision for your ideal business, but humour us. Imagine it.

Sit yourself at your desk in that future scene. What time is it? How did you get to the office? What's on your desk? What have you done today? Who have you spoken to?

Do you still do bookkeeping all day?

Hopefully you've answered no. Your role has become a strategic one – you plan what's next for your business, which services to offer, and which new team members you'll need. Heck, you might even be making plans to exit your business. You'll be supported by different teams or departments and you'll have managers running their own specialist areas, leaving you to guide the business.

> Your teams include a sales and marketing team, IT and accounts. You have a legal department and HR. And your business is run by a management team, of which you are a member.

And this should be the case no matter the size of your business. Whether you're a team of thirty or a team of one, you as a business owner need to have all of these departments. Right now, you probably run all of them as well. Even if you want to just do bookkeeping all day, you can't, no matter how small you keep your business. That's why we need to accept right now that our roles are more than bookkeeping, so we can set up our businesses effectively from day one. That means we can charge what we need to charge to make allowances for exactly what's involved in running a business. We need to take ourselves and our businesses seriously.

From this awareness that our businesses are more than us and that we may need to involve more people in building our business to its full potential than just ourselves, we can start to think about our business's departments and tasks so we can systemise, automate and outsource.

We believe that whether or not you want a team of employees, some level of outsourcing or delegation is the key to growth. If you're going to do what you do best, you need to not be distracted by "all the things". Think about how you can leverage your time to make your business most efficient and profitable. Checklists and procedures are your tools for successful delegation – they become your job descriptions. So start now.

Summary

In this chapter we've asked you to think about the foundations of your business and your legal structure. These are business essentials which need to be right from day one. We've also asked you to think about your business as a bigger entity than you might have imagined before.

Promoting yourself from the role of bookkeeping technician to CEO will help you build a mindset for growth and will set you up for success as we work our way through the rest of the book.

We know that the administration involved in starting a business can often be the reason bookkeepers don't get their practices started. The daunting task of applying for a practice licence, or the idea of stepping up and committing to being a business owner, can feel overwhelming.

Approach these tasks one at a time and reach out for support. If you're feeling you need help to move forward, we help bookkeepers to start a practice all the time through our Bookkeepers' Startup Programme. And our free 6 Figure Bookkeepers' Club community on Facebook is filled with bookkeepers who are on the same journey as you. Share your challenges and your successes with our group – we know there will be somebody else who is ready to help or who will be inspired by your progress, and we love to join these conversations.

IDEAL CLIENT

Yes you get a smaller slice of the pie.
But you get the whole slice!

~ Jo Wood

Chapter 2

FINDING CLIENTS

So, you're open for business!

And now you need some clients.

It can be tempting to take on any work that comes your way in the early days – you want to get experience and bring in some cash. We see bookkeepers throwing themselves into every networking event going, broadcasting on social media and feeling generally overwhelmed. We see some who don't know where to start so don't start, and others who make excuses not to look for clients because they lack the confidence to put themselves out there. In this chapter we're going to address the second part of our 5-step Framework, your ideal client. This might be a new way of thinking, so settle in and let's focus on finding the right clients for you.

Our worst clients

Can you think about the worst client or boss you've ever had? We think that being clear on why we don't enjoy working with certain people and businesses can help us feel much clearer about who we do want to work with and what we're looking for in an ideal client.

Zoe: I remember taking on a far-from-ideal client. There were a lot of red flags I should have noticed. He was using different software from any of my other clients. He had some very specific spreadsheets, and had been very clear in our first meeting that he was going to "eat my time". He'd told me to quote accordingly and said that I should use this as an opportunity to hire another member of staff. From the moment I met him, I had a bad feeling. But I also knew I could do what he needed. His spreadsheets weren't complicated, and I'd dealt with personalities like his before. So my first mistake was that I sent him a quote.

He negotiated hard on the quote. I was keen to be able to give a team member some extra hours so my next mistake was giving in to the reduced fee, and we started work.

I disengaged the client shortly after we started working together after he intimidated one of my staff.

Zoe's client was inflexible and acted inappropriately. She felt she should take him on to grow her business, and she felt thick-skinned enough to be able to handle him and his demands. But she also should have paid attention to the red flags at the first meeting, had respect for herself, and had the self-belief that it would be possible to find another client to give her team member those extra hours.

Jo: When I was in partnership with an accountancy firm, I was sent a lot of clients who had engaged with the accountancy practice and needed bookkeeping support. Bookkeepers are often advised to market to accountancy practices, but my experience is that you end up picking up the clients the accountancy practice simply doesn't want to service, which can make for a frustrating experience. The client in question was a shoe retail outlet that wasn't keeping the correct records. They'd ask me to file their VAT returns based on numbers they'd provided with no supporting evidence – which I refused to do. Alarm bells were ringing, and later, there was a VAT inspection during which the client became abusive.

Not every client is intimidating or abusive – some just don't appreciate what you're doing. Others always argue the bill, pay late or refuse to pay by direct debit, or want you to work Fridays even though you tell them you have childcare responsibilities that day. Others make you feel icky every time they phone you. If you're getting any of these warning signs, this client is not your ideal client. Note the red flags for future reference, discuss the challenge with your client, and if you can't find a solution, find another business to support instead.

Saying no to a client who is ready to pay is tough, particularly when you're trying to get your business off the ground. But you'll save yourself a lot of trouble if you know your values and can stick to your principles.

To be able to do this, you need to learn how you like to work and when you work, as well as which systems you like working with, which systems you don't, what is acceptable to you, and what isn't acceptable to you. We can't promise you won't have a difficult client ever again but you'll be in a much better place to grow a practice you feel is a joy to run.

Red and green flags

When we're able to define who we don't want for a client, we have a much better idea of who we do want. Over the years and through practice, we have learnt what feels good and what doesn't. We've both had clients who make us smile whenever we pick up the phone, clients we just love to help, and we know which clients will never cause us any trouble with payments.

But why is the relationship so different with those ideal clients than with the bad clients?

We are just as responsible for the good things that happen in our business as we are for the bad. So it's important to notice what is at play when a relationship isn't working well with a client so we can address whether something is wrong about the way we're working, the types of clients our marketing is attracting and the way we communicate.

We suggest taking a step back and trying to remove yourself from the emotion. Start to notice the energy around your conversations. Whether you find that your conversation ends with you feeling full of energy or leaves you feeling drained, it makes sense to tune into what made you feel that way.

* Was it the individual?
* Was it the project you were working on?
* Was it something connected to what the business itself does?
* Was it an external factor?

It can take time to tune in, but try to get into the habit of noticing the energy around your meetings and what you're doing. We find it best to trust our instincts when it comes to taking on clients.

Choosing a niche

No new business owner wants to rule out a huge population of clients that they could be working with, and the idea of niching and narrowing in on a particular group of potential clients can feel risky.

We need to make a very important point here before we move on. And this applies to every decision you will need to make about your business.

It is time to approach decisions with a view of abundance.

What do we mean by that?

Let's go back to something we've already spoken about: employment. Many of us will have worked as employees before starting our businesses. We're used to getting a fixed paycheck every single month. When we're conditioned in that way, we tend to have an overriding motivation to match or better our salary when we start a business. Everything we do is focused on finding clients who can match that income. We resist spending money because we feel we need to preserve every penny we can, and when we're doing that, we're telling ourselves that money is scarce, that money is limited and may run out. We tell ourselves our potential to get new clients is limited, and we tend to have a very fixed view of our potential. We think money is scarce and we assume our clients think in the same way.

Running a business is very different from being an employee. If nothing else, what we hope you learn from this book is that we are no longer in a transactional world of trading our time as an individual for money, an hourly rate, or a fixed pay check.

We'd love for you to see the opportunities of building something much more. We want you to leverage all the resources you have: your time, your reputation and your money. If you invest these "resources" in your business, you can build something so much greater.

We believe that identifying and serving a niche is a sensible strategy for a new bookkeeper because it's easier to build your reputation in one area, one industry or one skillset and to leverage your time (one of your critical resources) by becoming the go-to expert. It feels great to work with businesses in an industry you care about or know in detail. We know from helping bookkeepers we work with to become the go-to bookkeepers for particular industries that this can help you to quickly grow your business.

To allay a huge fear, we want you to know that when choosing a niche to target, you can still attract clients in all sectors. Fears about scarcity regularly surface when we talk to bookkeepers in our community about niching, but you won't need to turn away every business outside of your niche. You will simply benefit in two very significant ways:

1. You can become very targeted with your marketing and the time you spend networking. This means you can create a stronger brand with personality, rather than diluting how you put yourself out there by trying to speak to everyone. There is a saying that when you try to serve everyone, you serve no one, and we agree.

2. You become very efficient at serving your ideal client. You know their business, their challenges and the software they use inside out. This makes it easier for you to systemise your processes and build your business through automations and bringing in a team in the future.

Jo: I stumbled across my niche accidentally. When I started up my virtual FD business, I knew the services that I wanted to offer exactly. I also knew that my ideal client was most likely a female entrepreneur in her 30s, and probably a mother, but I wasn't necessarily sure in which industry she would work.

I went along to a monthly beauty appointment at a local salon and I was chatting away to the beautician who was working on me who mentioned the relationship she had with her accountant.

She was working with a traditional accountant, recommended by a relative, but she wasn't getting the support she needed. I felt really sorry for her. I started giving her some ideas about what could happen in her business if she made decisions herself based on what she knew about her industry, and we started to work together.

My beautician could not stop talking and singing my praises to everybody that she met, so much so that she was speaking to other beauticians that had salons. She was in a Facebook group of beauticians and hairdressers and salon owners and she was talking about how the experience that she'd had with me was so different from her traditional accountant. The person running the Facebook group then approached me and asked me to run some guest expert sessions, to speak to the group and create a workbook.

That group has grown to 400-plus salon owners, and that has been brilliant for my business. I accidentally stumbled into my niche, but it has allowed me to refine the services I offer, clearly target my marketing, and to build trust and receive recommendations and referrals.

Zoe: *My husband's a graphic designer so I'm naturally connected with a lot of creative professionals, many of whom are freelancers. My very first client, in fact, was a freelancer who'd asked me to do their tax return, and more work came to me after that through word of mouth. I took on clients in other industries as well, but where I lived, we had a thriving creative industry and it made sense to keep my focus there. I always go back to the economies of scale. Once you can deliver a service on a certain piece of software for one business of a certain size, you can deliver the same service over and over again for similar businesses of similar sizes using the same software in the same industry. Niching makes sense.*

Networks are smaller than we think. If there's an industry with which you have a natural connection, either through your work experience, your network or your interests, try to find the event that brings the businesses within that industry together – the networking group or conference. Even better if somebody at that event is already a happy client – you can become the expert in that room and you have a good opportunity to grow your client base.

Niching is a great way to develop a really targeted marketing campaign. You know who you're talking to and the industry they're in. You know about what's going badly for them at any given time, because you've got other clients going through the same thing. This means you can be really relevant as you speak to prospects and show that you understand what they're going through, because you know for sure what they're going through. You're speaking to people in this industry all the time, which gives you expertise that sets you apart.

> If you're struggling to identify your niche, think about who is already in your network: your current clients, organisations and clubs you're a part of, events you attend locally, your hobbies and your interests. Ask yourself whether there's a sector that would be a really good fit for you.

Many of the bookkeepers in our community have been able to pinpoint a niche after doing this piece of work. Several of our bookkeepers have decided to target eco and sustainable businesses as they have a personal interest in that area. Another bookkeeper works with online coaches and course creators, and another in the travel industry. Another niches in the equestrian sector. Some bookkeepers in our community have chosen to target businesses using a specific piece of software, businesses run by parents, or businesses in their local areas.

Jo: I have clients in multiple sectors who tend to come to me through word of mouth, but when I want to bring more clients into my business I target my marketing and focus on my niche. I know them and their pain points so well, I have a proven track record of success in the industry, so it's much easier to convert a prospect.

We believe that identifying a niche will help you build your business more quickly as you will have direction. Bookkeepers new to business can find the idea of niching scary when they look at it as restricting their opportunities rather than leveraging their time to increase their opportunities. We know that niching gives you an opportunity to attract the clients you can serve the best, and doing your best work makes for a great business and great referrals.

Working with accountants

Jo: *In the past, I created a niche of working with accountants. If I went to any networking events, I would go to accountants and talk to them about how I was a great bookkeeper. Over time, work would be referred to me. What I learned, however, is that the accountants were my clients, not the small businesses themselves. I never knew what kind of industry I'd be working with. One moment it could be someone who sold cakes, then it could be a football academy.*

It's true that I had a lot of clients, but I also had very little profit. I wasn't seen as the expert – the accountant was seen as the expert. This gave me very little scope to grow my practice except through volume of clients.

We still hear many bookkeepers who say they've been told to team up with accountants because it's a good way to get clients. In our experience, it's a good way to get a load of far-from-ideal clients, and we wouldn't recommend that as a route to market anymore. This is also a very difficult business structure to scale, as the accountant will likely want to pay you an hourly rate for your work. This means you're limited to how much work you can fit into your week, taking us back to the beginning of the book. Subcontracting for accountants usually means there's little margin available to make it worth growing your own team. One of our guiding values at The 6 Figure Bookkeeper is to help bookkeepers build businesses that work for them on their terms. We don't believe that working for accountants is the route to running your ideal business.

Summary

In this chapter we've thought about the industries and niches we like to work with. Perhaps we surprised you by telling you a bit about our worst clients, but understanding what you are definitely not looking for in a working relationship can be helpful in defining what it is that you need to grow a business you are passionate about.

We've got you thinking about your niche, and whether you'd consider working with an accountant. You don't have to have all the answers yet, and you'll pick up more ideas as we work through the rest of the book, but starting to explore who you want to be working with will help you make decisions about the services you're going to deliver. We'll look at these services in the next chapter.

SERVICE

A potential client told me they expected me to charge more because I am a specialist.

~ Kim Sones

Chapter 3

YOUR BOOKKEEPING SERVICES

What do bookkeepers do all day anyway?

If you're a member of any forums or Facebook groups for bookkeepers, you'll often see bookkeepers posting, asking how much to quote a client.

And you'll see answers ranging from a low hourly rate to a fixed package fee. We'll talk about pricing in a later chapter, but what we want you to understand from this chapter is how your services are an important factor in what you charge your clients. Getting your service offering right is so important to us, that this is the third part of the 5-step Framework we teach during our Bookkeepers' Bootcamp, read on to find out why.

Avoiding the low hourly rate game

If you want to avoid the low-hourly-rate game, you need to realise that your job is more than data entry. Clients will want to pay well for a bookkeeper who understands their business and their needs, but if they're used to receiving a poor or very light-touch once-per-year service, they might not know that's a possibility. Businesses pay well for someone who adds value to their business. That may be by solving problems or by helping them become more efficient and profitable. If you can be clear about what your clients need from you and how you can best serve them with the correct services, you can move away from seeing yourself as just a data-inputter and from charging a minimum wage.

In this chapter we're going to look at what your customers' pain points are, and how you can build the right services that bring value to your clients.

Customer pain points

Knowing your ideal client is the first step to selling a valuable bookkeeping service. To be able to bring value to our clients, we need to understand their pain points. This is easier when you know the specific client you are serving.

Business owners often think they want somebody to do "some data entry" for them – someone to "reconcile their bank" or "chase their invoices". But if you're able to have deeper conversations with your clients and prospects, you'll understand that what they really want is to feel more organised, to have more time, and to have more money in the bank.

If we really listen to our clients, we can build services that solve these problems. And we can market our services with messages that resonate with our ideal clients. We want our prospects to think, "Yes, that's what I'm feeling right now! This is what I need!"

Think back to Chapter 2 and the ideal client you identified, and put yourself in their shoes:

* When they first come to you, where are they likely to be on their journey?
* What difficulty will they most likely be experiencing?
* What is keeping them awake at night?
* What are their problems in business right now?
* What do their systems and processes look like?
* Where are they inefficient and frustrated?

Some business owners are struggling with time. The admin in their business is taking them away from making sales, from delivering products and services to their clients. Maybe they're so short of time that they're missing out on time with their families. They might be feeling swamped and overwhelmed, but afraid to delegate in case they lose control.

Some business owners feel afraid because the finances of their businesses have grown to become much more complex than when they first started. They're afraid of making a mistake or getting a fine from HMRC. This can create a lot of stress and anxiety for business owners, which can result in them feeling highly wound-up and creating complex spreadsheets and unnecessary processes to help them feel they're in control. Alternatively, they bury their heads in the sand and don't address the issue of their finances at all.

Other business owners have complicated relationships with money. It might seem crazy, but they may be afraid of having money, to the point that they're sabotaging their own businesses by overspending or holding themselves back from hitting the turnover they're really capable of.

Others do not want to spend on anything. They don't want to pay any tax, and they certainly don't want to pay for bookkeeping support. Getting inside the heads of these clients sets you up to see what they need from you, making you invaluable to them and their businesses.

> **Jo:** I took on a client called Kim who ran a beauty salon. She was doing really well in her business, her salon was beautiful and she was good with her clients, but I learned that she was petrified of the numbers. I realised from working with Kim that I love working with people who have this fear around numbers. That is where I can add the most value because I can hold their hand and say, "It's going to be OK – I'm going to help you". Then, what I like to do is build up their confidence, helping them set some goals, get clarity and build up systems that allow them to feel they have ownership of the numbers and actually feel that competence. I want them to be able to say, 'I understand my business, I understand the numbers.' That is my favourite thing.

Jo has built strong relationships with clients like Kim who need to build confidence around their numbers by having regular conversations and meetings.

Jo: I give her a weekly list of receipts we need. We're now down to two or three things every week, whereas at the beginning it was hundreds of items. It was a mess, but now we're right up to date. We always speak about the business, but we'll also talk about our lives and more spiritual things. Our conversations just fire me up – it's like talking to a friend. Who doesn't want to have clients that end up being friends?

There are people and businesses you will connect with better than others because you're on the same level. When you have a deep connection and can see your customers' pain points, you're able to understand them in a way that helps you give them what they need. That understanding is the key to creating amazing value.

Zoe: One of my first clients was a small design agency. They'd outgrown the level of support a family member had been giving them with their bookkeeping and were a bit behind. They'd just moved offices and had lost track of exactly what was going on in the business. Their accountant offered year-end compliance but not a monthly support package, and my client had a looming VAT deadline. Although on the surface it seemed the challenge was filing the VAT return, what they really needed was confidence they'd be able to pay the actual VAT bill. They didn't know what was happening with their cash flow.

It gave me great satisfaction to bring their accounting software up-to-date. That project helped crystallise the fact that I enjoyed working with small service-based businesses, and that my ideal client was probably most concerned about having his time back and confidence that any complexity was under control.

We're going to keep coming back to this message throughout the book, but if you are to avoid being a low-hourly-rate bookkeeper, you are going to need to differentiate yourself from the saturated market of bookkeepers charging on price. We have no doubt that if you aim to get work by being the cheapest bookkeeper in your sector or local area, somebody will undercut you.

> Knowing your customers' pain points will help you build the right services for a specific type of client with a specific set of needs. You won't be the ideal bookkeeper for every business, but for your ideal client, you will be the perfect bookkeeper. And that perfect fit is priceless.

We encourage you to identify a niche. Once you've done that, you can be incredibly targeted and so effective at serving that segment of the market because you understand them so well.

Standard bookkeeping services

Start-up bookkeepers often ask us what, exactly, a bookkeeper does from month to month, so it feels important to consider here the services that most bookkeepers provide.

Monthly bookkeeping

If you provide a monthly bookkeeping service, you will be completing all aspects of your clients' record-keeping up to reconciling the bank. As well as generally looking after their accounting system, this will likely include raising invoices, recording cash transactions, and recording purchases. Depending on whether you have access to the bank account, you might also be making payments.

This work may be completed on site or virtually. Many businesses that are too small to have an in-house finance team have this function performed by a bookkeeper who comes into the office for a set time each week. In other businesses, it will be the owner or a director completing the work. In our experience, bookkeepers are often called in when the director can no longer cope with the volume or complexity of the bookkeeping, or because their previous bookkeeper has moved on.

VAT

VAT is a complex area and many business owners are greatly comforted to know that an expert is handling their VAT affairs. If you submit VAT returns for your client, you will need to ensure their accounts are up to date at the VAT period end and that all transactions have the correct treatment and paperwork. You'll then prepare the VAT return and submit it after consultation with your client.

A good bookkeeper will keep a monthly 12-month rolling turnover of all of their clients. This is to ensure that the business owner can be informed when they are approaching the VAT threshold or if they need to change VAT scheme. Alternatively, their revenue might have reduced and they have the choice to deregister. Being able to offer your clients this insight is an extremely important part of your service, and advising on the types of schemes available and how they work raises you to expert status in their eyes.

Once your clients are VAT-registered, preparing and submitting their returns promptly gives a business owner enormous peace of mind. If you help them to save the money for their VAT monthly again, you are moving far away from the stereotype of a data entry clerk.

Payroll

Many bookkeepers provide payroll services. Payroll can be the largest expense a company has, so it is highly important that this service is completed in a timely and accurate manner. Over the years, payroll has become more and more involved, with RTI, auto-enrolment and managing furlough claims during the pandemic. You need to ensure that the business owner has the figures to pay staff as well as the amount owing to HMRC on a monthly basis. You will need to build a great relationship with the main point of contact as you will need to be informed of all joiners, leavers, holidays, sick leave and parental leave. Payroll is very involved, so many bookkeepers choose to outsource this service very early on in their business.

Tax returns

Many bookkeepers support clients with self-assessment tax returns each year. If you support a sole trader or partnership, they will need to complete these returns and you'll be best placed to complete them with their business's financial statements available to you. If you support limited companies, their directors will need self-assessment tax returns as well.

Depending on the complexity of the businesses and the individuals' finances, the work involved in completing a tax return can vary greatly. They can be as simple as entering earnings and tax already paid from different sources and confirming whether any tax is due to the client, or as complex as preparing a full set of accounts for a sole trader from his incomplete records.

Bookkeeping services you might not have thought of

Management reporting and budgeting

It's become popular to offer an advisory service that tends to include annual budgeting and cash flow forecasting sessions, as well as meetings throughout the year to support the business as it reflects on performance and plans for the future. Large organisations usually have in-house teams providing management accounting, and smaller businesses need support from somebody who is able to give them more insight into their business.

> There are huge opportunities to really add value to your clients' businesses by offering support with interpreting their financial data. As bookkeepers, we often underestimate our ability to do this.

When you go into any first meeting with a client, you might feel like they're interviewing you. Actually, we need to change the way we think about this as it is our opportunity to interview them. The reason you find yourself in a sales conversation with a potential client is usually because there's a problem somewhere in their business. It may be related to bookkeeping, or tax, or systems, and that is usually connected to a deeper challenge connected to their goals in business or life. They need to get their time back, they need certainty of their upcoming tax bill, and they need to plan for retiring from the business. That's why they've brought you in and you have the key – it's just that your conversation is probably at the surface level right now.

Conversations that lead to advisory services begin when you ask your clients about their challenges. Ask "What's happening for you right now? What are your plans?" A generic report for the sake of a report is not good management information. It is very difficult to sell this information when it doesn't have a purpose for the business owner.

Statistics and commentary that get a client closer to their goals, however, is good management information. If your client is going to see your value, you need to show them the information that will help them make the decisions that they care about.

Through management reporting, you can support your clients in setting and measuring key performance indicators. You can help them really understand their data and what's happening in their businesses so they can work towards their goals.

It can be as simple as starting with a sales target or working out how much the average customer spends with them. This data is incredibly powerful for a business owner who's never considered their average customer spend before, because if they can add an extra 1% or 10% per customer through increased prices, addons, repeat custom or subscriptions, it can completely change the course of their business.

Management reporting helps business owners answer the questions they have about their businesses, including how much they can take out and pay themselves, whether they'll be able to invest in staff, equipment and premises, and how their cash flow is looking.

We have this data at our fingertips. And when we niche, we can even benchmark our clients against each other. We can help our clients and we add value. We just have to believe it.

Workshops and training sessions

Offering workshops and training sessions might not be your first thought when you consider your service offering, but this can be a fantastic complementary service to your business. Workshops and training sessions offer the opportunity to provide services to several people at the same time, giving you a way to serve price-sensitive customers who might not be ready to pay for your regular services. They're a great way to leverage your time by providing one service to many people in one go, and they are a great way to demonstrate your credibility to prospects.

Workshops and training sessions have resulted in many referrals for us over the years. You might decide to cover basic accountancy training for small business owners, demonstrations of accountancy software, or sessions which answer your clients' specific challenges, from technical and regime changes through to business planning and credit control.

> **Zoe:** *Running paid workshops on basic finance skills for creative start-up businesses helped me find a lot of clients for end-of-year self-assessment. It also gave me a great opportunity to train them to keep accounting records in the best way to make my job easier at the end of the year.*

The right services for you

When designing your services, it's important to consider your training, your strengths and your interests. You'll be offering these services for a long time after all. You don't have to offer every service. You may choose to offer a selection of services or you may choose like Jo to offer a full end-to-end service.

> **Jo:** *I see every business owner as the CEO of a really large business. That means they should have an accounts department, and that's what we provide. We are the bookkeeper, the payroll team and the trusted financial director. At the end of every month, I meet my clients*

on Zoom to discuss future plans and what's happened in the last month, and to plan and budget. I hold them accountable, and I help them meet their financial goals.

Aligning services with client needs

So we've covered the list of services that we might be offering. And one of the essential parts of getting our service offering right, and the important point that most bookkeepers miss, is that we need to provide services that serve our clients' needs. And that means we need to understand our clients' emotions.

When your clients come to you, how are they likely to be feeling?

Now's the time for us to reflect on our findings from Chapter 2, because knowing your ideal client and understanding their pain points will help you deliver services which solve real problems, which add real value, and which result in very happy, satisfied customers.

If your client is feeling out of control, disorganised and worried, the best service for them will not only tick their boxes from a technical point of view, it will also give them confidence, reassurance and clarity. Confidence might be built by including training sessions or regular check-ins as you get your client organised and used to using a system. You can give reassurance by understanding which figures they need to understand to feel in control, ensuring they have an up-to-date dashboard with those figures at all times. You could help your client get clarity by working with them to understand their targets, setting some goals together, and checking in on them month by month.

We believe a great bookkeeper does so much more than just a great bank reconciliation, but we meet bookkeepers all the time who want to simply sit behind their computers, work away and get everything done – to be amazing at the operational part of being a bookkeeper. The thing we must understand is that if you want to be more than a bookkeeper, if you want to run a six-figure business, you can. But you need to offer a different level of service.

> And your business will stand out when you focus on communication.

Most businesses' only financial support comes from a meeting once a year with their accountants. They sit down and reflect on what happened in the last financial year, which probably ended more than six months prior to the meeting. As the people in touch with our clients' numbers every month, every week, we have an incredible opportunity to get to know them much better than this. By showing your clients you are interested in their business, by helping them set goals and focus on the numbers that are important, as well as to get so much more out of the data, you can create strong relationships that make you so much more valuable than a data entry clerk.

And if you believe you're just not skilled enough or experienced enough to provide that level of support, then you need to know this.

You already have all the data you need at your fingertips. The great bank reconciliation you've completed gives you an incredible amount of insight into the business. You will add value when you know how to communicate the insight your clients need from that data.

Do you want to know a secret?

Being able to understand your clients' goals, hopes and dreams, and helping them interpret the numbers in a way that can support them to achieve what they want, not just in business but in life, is the difference between an hourly-rate bookkeeper and a six-figure bookkeeper.

Next time you're sitting at your computer, search for "bookkeeping services" in your browser. You will find numerous bookkeepers whose business model is built on clients posting paperwork to them, then recording the transactions and getting tax returns filed. Consider those bookkeepers for a moment and ask yourself this:

How much should business owners expect to pay for a service like this?

The only way to deliver this service profitably is to minimise contact and minimise the opportunities to really get to know your clients. Do you think the bookkeeper has time to provide a personalised service to these clients?

Interestingly, one of the reasons we think so many bookkeepers fail to build a very profitable business is that they don't see this. They want to provide more support, but they're afraid to charge for it. This leaves them working too many hours for not enough money, creating the impression that bookkeeping is a poorly paid, poorly valued service. But we do this to ourselves.

It is not possible to charge for a really good, hands-on, personal service when you're simply processing data and posting pieces of paper around. And that's because you are not providing a valuable personalised service. The only way to make this type of service profitable is to highly automate it and never intend for it to be a personalised service. You need to be able to deliver it cheaply.

People receiving this type of service will of course still get their accounts and tax returns filed by the deadline, and you can build a profitable business doing this if you design your business in the right way, but do you think your clients will be any the wiser about how their businesses are performing?

We believe that bookkeepers have an opportunity to become experts for their clients. When we support our clients with a level of service they never thought possible, we are able to stand out against the backdrop of cheap, volume-based services.

This means we need to move from providing a tick list service to providing an insightful, supportive package that helps our clients to meet their goals. Large organisations have finance teams and business partners supporting service managers with their roles, ensuring they feel in control of their budgets, understanding where they're heading, and keeping them accountable. Seeing ourselves as finance managers and finance directors is where we as bookkeepers can make sure we're positioned to do the same.

Jo: "When I started my practice, I built a month-end checklist, which I used for every client. It started off very simple with everything that you would usually expect: making sure the bank reconciliation was done, making sure all the sales invoices were posted, making sure the Dext account was cleared and so on. I scheduled monthly calls with my clients, and rather than just telling them about their bank reconciliation, I asked them what they were worried about in their businesses. If they brought something up, I'd add it to their month-end checklist as something to check in on every month – a KPI, if you like.

"Some of the smaller clients who are growing worry about VAT registration, so I added a VAT checker for every client who wasn't already VAT-registered as a standard check for each month.

"These checklists start a conversation and help my clients hit their targets. They finally feel in control of their finances."

Perfecting the design of your own bookkeeping practice will take time and practice. Our advice to you is to see what works, ask questions and see where you get the best feedback on your services. Then systemise your best way of working and roll that out across all of your clients so they always receive this same amazing service.

The personal journey with our clients is the key to truly adding value. This isn't just about business – it's about personal goals and dreams. We have to remember that our role isn't just to process some transactions. Our role is to identify our clients' pain points, to deliver technically excellent bookkeeping, and to take our clients on a journey to the place they want to be. Your services will be different depending on the clients you work with and your particular strengths. There's no right or wrong, and differences will stand out.

Next time you speak to a client, why not ask them about their business and personal goals? Think about how what you do can help them in the pursuit of these goals. Remember just as you're setting up your business now, your clients did the same. They have goals, dreams and aspirations for their businesses as well. Once you are able to open up conversation lines, you start to become a vital part of their business.

How communication improves your service

Have you ever been told that in ten years' time there won't be any bookkeepers or accountants because technology will replace us?

It's true that technology, software and apps can do a lot more of what we used to do, but we don't need to see this as a threat.

The threat is that we fail to speak to our clients any more because we rely on technology too much. And as technology allows us to do our jobs more efficiently and effectively, we need to recognise the opportunity we have to deliver data to our clients in a way they understand because we actually have time to do so.

When we think of ourselves as a substitute for technology and computers, we see ourselves purely as data inputters and we underprice. It is impossible to see our value when we believe we can be replaced by a bit of software. Instead, we need to see that the opportunity technology gives us is a role where we have time to interpret that data and prepare information in a way that supports our clients. This allows clients to make better choices and move their businesses towards their goals. And that's where the magic happens. That's where we add value. This is why communication – the human aspect of what we do – is so important.

Jo: During the first lockdown of the pandemic, I set up a Facebook group for my clients because I was being asked the same questions all the time about the coronavirus loans and furloughing. I set the groups up for my clients and I was then able to give them information as soon as it came out via posts and videos.

If your clients are on Facebook, and if they respond to video in groups, you can do that too. If your clients are out and about and respond to text messages, you could use a text service to communicate important points and deadlines to them. Knowing your ideal client will help you identify the best communication methods.

Your ideal client is different from the ideal client of the next bookkeeper (in fact the "next" bookkeeper may not even know who their ideal client is), and that's why we believe bookkeepers should design a service that is right for their clients.

You can then decide on how many touchpoints you're going to have with your clients. Once you've decided, you can put the process in place that makes sure your service operates in the way you want it to. It's easy to say, "I'll be so much better than that traditional firm down the road", but we guarantee that without setting the intentions and designing the systems, once you get busy, communication can be the first thing to slip.

Zoe: "*I always found that if a client asked me a question on an email, maybe about something they're stuck with or frustrated about, I got great results by recording a quick video response as I worked through their question. Taking time to record a video showed that I had taken the time to think about my client. It helped them feel empowered to sort the issue out themselves next time, and they also got to know me better.*

Summary

In this chapter, we've looked at the standard bookkeeping services you might expect to offer as well as our more unique takes on what a bookkeeper can offer. We think it's important to really understand your ideal client and to discover what their pain points are, so you can deliver services that actively solve their problems. You can stand out from the crowd when your clients see you supporting them through their specific challenges, so we've looked at aligning your services with your client needs to make you the best bookkeeper for your clients' businesses.

Chapter 4

YOU'RE WORTH MORE

How much should a bookkeeper charge per hour?

Zoe: *I was hired by one of my first clients because they were behind in reconciling Xero, and I'd been recommended by somebody they knew. My bookkeeping business was a side-hustle and I was still employed in my job as a finance manager in the insurance team of a large bank. I knew I had the technical knowledge to do what the client needed from me, but I had no idea how to charge.*

I Googled "bookkeepers in Bristol" and decided I might be worth anywhere between £10 and £30 per hour. As an accountant I thought I was probably towards the top of the scale, but I wasn't very experienced as a bookkeeper and went in at £25 per hour. Compared with my employed salary it seemed about right, but I winced when I told the client the price. Fortunately, they agreed to pay me.

I was charging them a few hundred pounds every month, but as time went on, I realised that as I'd improved their systems and saved myself time, I was being paid less and less each month. I was also providing way more in terms of service than the data entry they had hired me for. I'd helped them with tricky credit control challenges and reclaimed VAT they didn't even know they could recover. I also hadn't factored in the cost of the software I was using in my business, the extra hour it took me to travel to their office when we met in person, or any other business overheads.

It became clear that I needed to find a better way to charge.

The hourly rate trap

An important consideration for your service is how much you sell it for. How to price bookkeeping services is without question the thing we are asked about more than anything else in The 6 Figure Bookkeepers' Club.

By now you'll be starting to realise that you are worth as much as the value you are providing to your clients. You might be starting to see that there are opportunities to add more valuable services than you originally thought.

We also know that you might still be experiencing some doubts, and unsure of how else to price, you'll probably be tempted to quote a low hourly rate or offer the client a discount.

But our question at the start of this chapter was a trick question.

When you charge an hourly rate for your work, you are commoditising yourself. You are making yourself interchangeable with somebody else who can provide the same service, so when somebody cheaper comes along who can also do their bookkeeping, your client is going to drop you for the cheaper option.

This is how bookkeepers stay in the low hourly rate trap.

It's time to stop seeing yourself as just "another bookkeeper", only worth a low hourly rate. It's time to remind yourself of those customer pain points in Chapter 3 so that you can offer a service that is worth more.

> Your aim can't be to simply offer several hours of data entry and processing. Instead your goal must be about transformation for your clients.

Zoe: A few months ago, Vicky got in touch with me. I know her from a networking event and she asked whether I could recommend somebody to 'do her accounts'. She's in the creative sector and I gave her a few recommendations. Vicky came back to me and asked me 'Would you say that £160+VAT per month was fairly standard? It's so hard to know how much to expect to pay but it sounds a lot.'

It was obvious to me that what Vicky had left the sales conversation with was simply the price. She hadn't understood the value for her business of working with that particular bookkeeper or firm - price was the key factor, and that's why she'd come back to check with me.

We're so used to the idea of getting three quotes and choosing the best, but unless there's anything else to lead on, "best" will simply come back to "cheapest". There was an opportunity for whoever spoke to Vicky to demonstrate how they'd helped businesses just like hers to hit their goals and to help her with whatever her concerns were about business, but that opportunity had been missed. Whether they got Vicky's work or not probably came down to the price in the end. We need to break that cycle.

The sum of your knowledge and experience

When you set out to train as a bookkeeper, you will have started on a journey of education and knowledge building.

Numbers are probably your thing – we expect your love of numbers and of getting people organised is the reason you've decided to set up your bookkeeping business.

Your love of and comfort with numbers means training as a bookkeeper, however difficult you've found it, came more easily to you than it would to other people – those who don't choose bookkeeping for a profession themselves. And even if you have found it incredibly easy, that does not mean your job is easy, and it doesn't mean what you do is of low value.

You've done years of training. You have years of life and work experience. You've also benefited from the years of training and experience of those who have trained you, so what you bring to each piece of work you do for your clients is the sum of yours and others' years of training, knowledge and experience.

We guarantee you that bookkeeping is worth more than the minimum wage, and we hope you can see this too.

Pricing

So it's time to raise the bar. We as bookkeepers aren't going to comoditise ourselves and compete on price. So where do we start with pricing?

We are hardwired to come at business from a point of lack: the belief that clients are scarce and if we don't win this piece of work we will struggle to find another client. We therefore tend to benchmark our "value" against other bookkeepers, always trying to ensure our charges are "reasonable" to our clients. When we see our value, we see that our fees are more than "reasonable" for the results we give, so we need to consider whether our charges are "reasonable" to ourselves.

Hourly Rate Pricing

The majority of bookkeepers still charge an hourly rate. When you start your bookkeeping practice, particularly if you've come from a background of employment, you're most likely to assume you need to charge an hourly rate.

We've seen bookkeepers in the UK charging anything from £10 per hour upwards. We've had conversations with accountants who charge £80 or more per hour. For the purposes of benchmarking, it's useful to know that if what you take home (after your business overheads, after your software, after tax) is within this range, then you're making a good start. But we're frustrated that the majority of bookkeepers are right at the bottom of this range. In fact, that's why we felt we should write this book.

> We help bookkeepers start profitable bookkeeping practices that work for them. We want bookkeepers to run businesses that give them financial security and the flexibility they need. And we know that both of these things are difficult to achieve when you're charging a low hourly rate.

If you're just processing data, it's going to be difficult to compete with fellow bookkeepers on anything other than price, leaving you in the low hourly rate bracket. But not all bookkeeping hours are created equal. If you're highly experienced and productive and do what you do in such a way that your client is streamlined, efficient and set up to gain a level of insight into their numbers that they'd never had before, then you can charge more than somebody who's just processing data. The insight you can give is the valuable piece of the service for your client. If you only charge on processing transactions, there's never an incentive to work more quickly or to automate anything you do.

Let's bring it back to your alternative.

Your alternative to going into business is to have a paid job. So one place to start with pricing is to consider what you'd earn if you were employed. In fact, we ask the bookkeepers who work with us to go through this exercise.

So factor in your overheads and the non-chargeable time you spend doing administrative work, taking sales calls, marketing and training. Then factor in the breaks and holidays you'll need to take occasionally. Consider the fact that you might occasionally be sick. You'll soon see that you need to charge a much higher hourly rate than you originally thought.

This can be a tough exercise if you've been charging a low rate for a long time. It's certainly incredibly eye-opening. And we urge you to ask yourself: if you're going to be a lot better off in a job, why are you running a business right now?

We think it's clear that we don't favour an hourly rate, but once you are aware of what would be a minimum acceptable hourly rate, you can challenge your prices from a place of objectivity. We want you to know the minimum you should be earning for the time you're working so you can make better decisions about everything related to pricing going forward. It's easy when you're passionate about what you do to let your work consume you, to do people favours, to log in late to get that thing finished off. But think back to Chapter 1 when we challenged you to see yourself as the CEO of your large business. Do you think that large business can scale if it doesn't charge effectively?

Charging a low hourly rate is where many bookkeepers start off on the wrong foot in business. They forget about the administrative time and overheads involved in running a business. Their low hourly rate means that once everything else involved in running a business is factored in, they take home less than the minimum wage.

We have bookkeepers in our community who weren't paying themselves at all when they started working with us. It's time to make a change.

Fixed Pricing

One of the challenges for us and our clients when we charge an hourly rate is that neither they, nor we know what their bill is going to be when we get to the end of the month. These kinds of fluctuations make it very difficult to budget and to plan your time from month to month, not to mention the impact on your family finances of moving from feast to famine from one month to the next. Asking clients to buy blocks of hours in advance doesn't work either, because if they don't have time to provide the information you need to do your work, you're simply pushing those hours out into the future, further increasing your lumpy cash flow.

If you want to scale your business in any way, you need to have some guarantees over your earnings so you can build and monitor a budget.

In a world where we live by the clock, planning our days, our mornings and our lunch breaks, it is difficult to get away from thinking of our time in hours. We think ultimately that most pricing methods have some kind of proxy for units of time, whether that means charging for the time itself or charging for a volume of transactions.

> Fixed pricing may well have its foundations in the time involved, but it gives you a stable base to resource and build your business from.

There is software on the market that has been designed to help bookkeepers and accountants quote a fixed price rather than by the hour. GoProposal, for example, builds proposals for clients based on the size of their businesses or the number of transactions they conduct, using a rate card or a cost per transaction to create a transparent pricing method, with the option to add and remove services.

Jo: There's something about seeing the detailed proposal on screen that justifies the price to the client. If I take on a job with a few months of catch-up work, I can make sure those extra months are charged for so I don't lose out. It's very transparent, my clients can see exactly what I'll be doing for them, and they'll also see that they're going to get the same price as another client. There's no special treatment; it's fair."

Having a fixed price in place also means you're incentivised to look for efficiencies in the work you do. You're still paid the same no matter how quickly the work is completed. If you're paid by the hour, this isn't the case.

We recommend that if you charge fixed rates, you schedule a fee review every quarter and make that part of your contract with your client.

Your Profitable Approach

Throughout our programme for bookkeepers, The Bookkeepers' 6 Month Success Programme, we challenge bookkeepers to consider their life goals and the earnings that would help them achieve those goals.

> Knowing how to charge is a wonderful thing, and you may well have a goal of matching or bettering your salary as an employee. Getting your pricing right is fundamental to doing this.

But imagine if there could be more?

We believe you started your business because you want more from life. Maybe you want flexibility to work around your family, to take the summer holidays off, or to travel whenever you want to. Maybe you need to work around health appointments or the care of a loved one.We know you can build a profitable business that allows you to do that.

But often we're so used to being employees, to working 9–5 in an office for an hourly rate and having our holidays scheduled around the needs of a business rather than our own lives, that it can be a challenge to think bigger.

It's OK to think bigger. This is your business, after all, and we think goals give you a great sense of direction and allow you to make decisions with purpose.

Without goals, you simply can't know what you're working towards and you'll simply be at the mercy of opportunities that happen to come your way rather than seeking them out.

Goal setting takes courage, but once you know what you're aiming for, you can start to consider what you need to earn to support the lifestyle you're working so hard for. Those earnings represent the profit after tax you need to target in your business, giving you the beginnings of some clear financial goals for your business.

It takes bravery to think bigger than earning an hourly rate, or to think bigger than replacing your salary from employment, but daring to identify your goals and using that insight to set financial targets will help you build your bookkeeping practice for success.

Here's what we recommend you do:

With your goals in mind, and with a financial sum attached to those goals, we want you to consider what your business would need to look like to achieve what you've set out. You might need to think differently about how you build your business than you've thought about it so far. Nothing is off limits when you design this business.

Let's say your goal is to generate £100,000 of net profit for your business and you want to take school holidays off.

What does your business need to look like to get there?

Do you lead with a low-cost tax return service? This is definitely a route you could take, and this is going to be a volume game. You're unlikely to physically have the capacity to do all of the tax returns yourself. This means your business will need to be highly systemised with automations. Maybe your marketing is built around Facebook advertising that sends potential clients to a website. Maybe your communication is only virtual and you're staffed by a team who can support that style of business model.

At the other extreme, you might decide to position yourself as a high-value bookkeeping team offering bespoke services to growing businesses in a specific field that are working towards specific targets. You'd be staffed by a team that could deliver certain aspects of client work, with you supporting clients in specific meetings. You'd lead your marketing through your business brand, taking speaking engagements, maybe running your own YouTube channel or podcast.

We often forget that we get to choose how our business looks and operates, and the next step is to design the business that's right for you. You could have 100 clients who pay you £1,000 per year, you could have ten clients who'll pay you £10,000 per year, or you could have something in between.

These are completely different business models, each of which could help you achieve your goal.

We guarantee it will be easier to find and manage ten clients than it will be to find and manage 100, but if systems and automation are your passion, a lower value offering might well be your preference. We simply want you to see that you get to choose, but you need to ensure that the choice you make is profitable.

The opportunity is there for you when you can see it.

Getting paid

Jo: For years and years, I would do the work and have a timesheet, and raise an invoice at the end of the month, and then I would give my clients 30 days to pay. They'd never pay on time.

If we're not being paid ourselves, what sort of bookkeepers can we be for our clients?

It's important here for us to talk about getting paid. Cash flow is vital for every business, so let's get this right from the start.

The simplest way to ensure your monthly bookkeeping clients pay you on time is to sign them up for direct debit and to bill them monthly in advance.

This takes courage. You might have to overcome feelings of imposter syndrome and you're going to have to believe that you're worth the value you are going to add for your clients before you've even done the work. We'd like you to know, however, that this is standard practice across the industry and the best way to guarantee you will be paid for the work you're about to do. A direct debit can be set up simply at the point of engaging with the client.

The process is a little different for one-off services, but it is still a straightforward way to ensure you are paid for your work. With tax returns and project jobs, you can take the approach of holding off filing an important document or return until payment is received – you might choose to exercise some discretion if you're right on the deadline. Alternatively you could consider asking your clients to book and pay for some services upfront online, or invoicing your clients a percentage of their fee in advance before you commence work.

Summary

In this chapter we've considered why bookkeepers fall into the low hourly rate trap. We've given you some methods to help you assess the correct hourly rate for your work. We've discussed how you can build that out into a fixed fee, and then we've looked at engineering profitable services that help you take a strategic approach to achieving your earning goals, rather than being at the mercy of any client you can find.

ENGAGE

People buy from people who they know,
like and trust.

~ Ashley Leeds

Chapter 5
NETWORKING EVENTS

Zoe: I knew I needed to do some marketing soon after I launched my bookkeeping practice. I had a few clients, which I'd gained through word of mouth, but I knew I'd need to make a conscious effort if I really wanted to grow. I searched online and came across a website that promised to match prospects with bookkeepers.

The idea was that small business owners looking for a bookkeeper would fill in a form online giving their contact details and a few facts. The website would send a summary of that information to bookkeepers in the local area, and if I wanted the business owner's contact details, I'd spend the 'credits' I'd purchased to be able to quote for the job.

I spent hours quoting for jobs and never heard back from any of the prospects – it was a waste of time and money. Even now, I probably still have some unused credits.

To succeed in business, you're going to need clients and in the next part of the book, we're going to help you market your business and find clients. It's all about engaging with the right people - the E in our 5-step Framework, but without the reset, the ideal client and the service clearly defined, bookkeepers can get stuck at this point.

They tell us they can't find clients because their sales skills need work, but we know that bookkeeping is a much needed skill, so in this section we'll discover what you can do to find the clients you need and start and grow your practice.

Although there are websites and directories, we know that you'll be better at finding the right clients for your business when you align your marketing efforts with your ideal client. We'll explore social media and PR later, but in this chapter, we're going to dig into the go-to marketing tool for so many: networking.

Networking events

One of the ways bookkeepers often look to find clients is through business networking events. Lots of small business owners in a room, swapping business cards: it sounds like the perfect place to find clients, doesn't it? But like many of the bookkeepers in our community, you might identify with being an introvert. Being in a room full of people you've never met might well be your worst nightmare.

The second pitfall we often run into is that if you've ever Googled networking events, you might have become overwhelmed by the range of members-only events, breakfast networking events, expos and women's networking. If you're even going to find the courage to attend, where do you start?

Luckily, if you've reached this point in the book, you've already given your ideal client a lot of thought. This will help you to start your research. A word of warning: not every event is going to be right for you, and taking a scattergun approach is going to be a frustrating waste of time.

Choosing the right event

So it's time for a reminder. Who is your ideal client?

Networking takes time out of your day: finding the event, checking your diary, getting to the event, meeting people and following up. Some networking events will also require you to refer work to others, which again takes your time.

Being clear on who you should be networking with will ensure you only find yourself at events that are worthwhile, making you more effective at using your time. If your ideal client happens to be someone who works locally to you, a local group could be the right place to network. But if the only local group you can attend is for mothers in business and your ideal client is a 50-year-old man who runs an IT company, you're going to be in the wrong place. Being targeted and choosing the right events to attend is important.

Right now, one of the best places to find events is a website called Eventbrite. If you have a specific target market – for example if your ideal client is part of a specific community, a certain industry, or a member of a particular association, attending events they'll be attending makes sense and will save you time.

Your ideal client is going to determine the type of event you choose to attend, so you might be looking for a lunchtime event during term time to connect with female business owners in the wellness space or you might find yourself attending an evening talk and networking event for tech start-ups.

We recommend asking your existing clients which events they attend. If you go along to an event where you already have a happy client who will sing your praises, they'll do a lot of your selling for you as well.

What to expect

We've attended many breakfast networking sessions between us. These events usually start with coffee and some free networking, followed by breakfast. There is usually networking amongst your tables of six or eight people with an opportunity to pitch. You might then find that some people move to other tables to allow the attendees to mingle throughout the event in a systematic way.

Lunches and evening events work in similar ways, sometimes incorporating a speaker or with a regular attendee having the opportunity to make a presentation on their expert subject.

Jo: I think going to a physical group is a really good idea if you've never done it. If you've never had to stand up and pitch yourself, you'll take great value from the learning experience of perfecting that introduction, not to mention being forced to get out from behind your computer.

How to prepare

For physical events like this, we'd recommend that you are prepared to make a 60-second introduction. 60 seconds isn't as long as you think – it gives you time to read about 150 words, which is less than half an A4 page of text. You should include:

* ⋆ Who you are
* ⋆ What you do
* ⋆ A fact that will get people's attention
* ⋆ Who you want to connect with
* ⋆ How people can connect with you

If you've ever sat at that breakfast table waiting for your turn to pitch, you'll know that you're not really listening to the other people, particularly if this is your first time. You're actually rehearsing what you need to say when it's your turn and hoping you don't mess up your words.

Your attention-grabbing fact and your statement about who you want to connect with is important for this reason. It's your opportunity to tell the people in the room why they should connect with you and how to do that.

Think very carefully about what you want to achieve at that event – a Key Performance Indicator for yourself if you like. Is it that there's a particular person coming along who you want to connect with? Or are you looking

> to connect with a specific number of people who can introduce you to small business owners who want to outsource their bookkeeping?

It's important to make sure you have a way for people to connect with you afterwards. You might think you need perfect business cards before you go networking, but people lose business cards. What people don't lose is emails. So don't let your lack of business cards stop you networking and making connections. Just ask for your new contact's email address and send them a quick email there and then with the subject, Hello. You can then follow up after the event.

Other types of events

Another way to get introductions to businesses is to attend conference-style or seminar-type events for the industry or group you work with. If your ideal clients are in the beauty industry, for example, attending a beauty-related exhibition could be a very good move. If you're interested in working with people in the sustainability space, attend a seminar about the new congestion charge being brought into your local city centre.

These sorts of events could be conferences or training with a guest speaker, but they almost always have the opportunity for networking with a coffee or glass of wine at the start or end of an event. If you've just seen an interesting talk, you already have a conversation starter. You won't need to formally pitch, but be ready to tell people what you do and make sure you work the room so you can introduce yourself to as many people as possible.

Online events

Physical groups have moved online since the pandemic and this has opened up opportunities for bookkeepers to network in a wider geographic area than they might have before. If you work within a niche sector with few ideal clients on your doorstep, this is a huge opportunity.

Events organisers have made a great effort to make online events work like in-person events. We certainly love online networking events because there's no travel time. Whereas an in-person event might take up three hours of your day once you include travel, you can be in and out of a Zoom meeting within an hour. We also love that when meetings aren't challenged by geography, we benefit from a wide range of speakers and a wider range of attendees. We love that online meetings can give us the opportunity to extend our reach and meet people we just wouldn't meet otherwise.

Format of online networking events

The format of an online networking event will depend on the organiser's preferences and, to an extent, their creativity. Most take the same format each week or month.

They will usually start with an introduction from the organiser and the opportunity for each attendee to briefly introduce themselves. There's sometimes an icebreaker, which could be a game in smaller groups which the organiser will send into breakout rooms. Alternatively, you might be asked to share something in the chat or to hold up a piece of paper displaying a key word, a drawing, or even a household object.

There will be a main part of the event, and this is usually some training or a talk from an expert within the group or a guest speaker who brings expertise in something the rest of the group lacks or has requested training in.

Some groups have smaller breakout sessions to discuss certain topics, which could be related to the theme of the day's event, and within these smaller groups there's usually a better opportunity for group conversation or speed networking.

How to approach an online event

We prepare ourselves for online networking events in just the same way as we would for an in-person event. It's important to know the purpose for you of attending that event, to be ready to start conversations and ready to pitch.

With an online event there is of course the benefit of being able to have notes without them being as obvious as when you're attending in person, and if you're new to networking, it can be reassuring to have the key points of your pitch in front of you. It can also be helpful to make notes of attendees you want to connect with after the event, or even to connect on social media while you're still on the call.

How often to go networking

Networking is part of a marketing strategy for many bookkeepers, and the amount and type of networking you choose to do will depend on where your ideal clients can be found, your goals, and your plans for growth.

Attending two or three different local networking events over the course of a few weeks can help you to get known in your area, particularly when you keep bumping into the same people. Although it may seem counterintuitive to network with the same people more than once, trust is built over time. The more conversations you can have, the more likely you are to get beyond surface-level discussions, allowing trust to deepen. Investing time with a small network that has the right connections could potentially be a very good move for your business

Networking is important, but it can take up a lot of time, particularly when you're doing it in person. If you enjoy networking, it can be tempting to go to everything on offer. We recommend that once you've got the lie of the land and understand which events work for you, you can choose your events strategically. You may then choose to commit to becoming a member of one specific group, but we suggest you try other events occasionally to extend your reach.

Being the guest expert

As we've mentioned, many events have a guest expert or speaker as the "main act". Speakers might have between 20 and 30 minutes on stage to talk about a subject of interest to the room, and you'll have the opportunity to hear from a fantastic range of experts when you start to attend networking events. If you see that there's an expert speaker who you think will specifically appeal to your ideal client, then the event they're speaking at would be a great event to attend. Better still –what if you were the guest speaker?

Having a "guest expert" slot at a networking event, whether virtual or in person, is an incredible way to raise your profile and to build trust and credibility. If you can get yourself invited along to an event attended by your ideal clients, you will have a fantastic opportunity ahead of you.

Imagine having the opportunity to speak to a room full of potential clients about your expertise.

If you find yourself in this situation or have the opportunity to pitch yourself as a speaker, to ensure you add value and make an impact, we suggest you deliver a presentation that addresses your clients' pain points. Showing up not just as an expert but as someone who has solutions will give a huge boost to your reputation.

Let's set some expectations here. It's unlikely that you'll be considered for a guest speaker slot from your first meeting, but if you think there's an overlap between your expertise and what the audience at that event needs, attend the event a few times and get a feel for who goes along. Study the topics of interest to the audience, understand the format of the speaker slots, get to know the organisers, and make your pitch to them at the right time.

How to be confident when out of your comfort zone

Many of the bookkeepers in our community are introverts and can't think of anything worse than going into a room full of people they don't know and reciting a 60-second pitch.

We know that building confidence in these situations takes practice – we've felt those nerves too. Our advice is to:

* Choose events which you think will attract ideal clients
* If you're unsure, reach out to the organiser beforehand to find out about the format of the event
* Prepare your pitch, and practise
* Try an online event first if it helps you build confidence. It's very easy to leave if you're not enjoying it.
* Attend an event where you already have a contact if this will put you at ease

Talking to people is essential for building your business and you can do this.

What to do after a networking event

Networking and free breakfasts are great, but one of the most important parts actually happens once the event has finished, and that is the following up.

If you have connected with somebody and had a good conversation, the simplest thing to do is to book a discovery call with them then and there or send an email after the event. You could also connect with them on social media and, provided you have their consent, and subject to GDPR rules, add them to your mailing list so you can stay in touch with them in the future.

LinkedIn may be a natural place to connect as it's the business platform of choice for most small business owners. Rather than firing off a simple connection request, consider personalising your invite with a couple of sentences that describe what stood out about the event you attended, some common ground or a specific reason you thought it would be great to stay in touch.

If your ideal client is more likely to be on another platform, then connect with them there and engage with some of their content. You could even make sure your notifications are turned on for their posts so that you're prompted to build that particular relationship.

Summary

When you start your bookkeeping business, attending networking events is a brilliant way to build your network and raise awareness of what you do. We think that using networking events well as part of your networking strategy can be extremely worthwhile. We know how daunting it might feel if you've never been networking before, but we also know that attending the right events can reap rewards.

Our advice is to keep it simple. Don't take a scatter-gun approach to networking. Instead, we'll bring you back to finding the communities your ideal clients belong to so you can build your confidence amongst like-minded people who could potentially become clients. Rehearse your pitch and don't overthink it. Everyone in that room or on that video call once went to their first networking event too, and many felt exactly as you do about it. You've got this.

Chapter 6

ONLINE MARKETING

Imagine you've been recommended to your ideal client by a mutual contact. Do you think they're going to pick up the phone straight away?

Put yourself in their shoes. What would you do? You might well pick up your phone, but would you actually call them? If you're anything like us, you'd probably search for them online instead.

If your client is most likely to try and find out more about you by looking online, the place you're going to need a presence is – you've guessed it – online.

In this chapter we'll help you find your home online. Potential clients want to find out everything they need to know in an online search, so it's time to talk about your website, your social media presence and your online PR strategy.

Websites

You're fairly unlikely to start your business with an office on day one, let alone a high street presence. Few business owners expect to walk down the high street and happen upon a bookkeepers' office.

These days, websites are considered shop windows, just on the internet instead of the high street. And we believe the virtual world gives bookkeepers a fantastic opportunity to compete with traditional firms on the high street when they get their messaging spot-on for their ideal client.

> A good website tells your ideal client that you're the right bookkeeper for them. It does that by showing that you're skilled and experienced. It should show your ideal client that you serve clients like them, and that you sell services that solve their problems.

You'll be aware that most businesses have websites. More and more bookkeepers have websites, and you're probably already convinced that you need one too, but here are two words of caution. Websites are one of the biggest stumbling blocks for bookkeepers in our community, preventing them from moving forward in two ways:

1. Bookkeepers think they need a website when actually utilising social media could be enough to get them started. They let not having a website become an excuse not to look for clients or build their businesses – because they don't have anywhere to "send them".

2. Alternatively, bookkeepers do have a website but it doesn't talk to the type of client they want to work with. The website might be badly built or it might not be

representative of who they are. Maybe it can't be found or is not helping potential clients to find out enough of what they need to know to take action or to become clients.

You don't have to have a website, but lack of websites and poor websites stop bookkeepers we work with from moving forward. We have accountability calls with bookkeepers on our Bookkeepers' 6 Month Success Programme every week, and somebody regularly attends and tells us they're joining to be held accountable for building or updating their website.

Perhaps you're starting to question the cost of a website right now and we're not suggesting you invest thousands of pounds in web design. We do, however, believe that once you get a decent website, you are most likely to be found in the most popular way, internet search, and have a "home" on the web where potential clients have almost all the information they need before they speak to you on the phone. If you make it clear that you have the solution for your ideal client's challenge, they might well have already decided they want to work with you by the time you speak to them on the phone.

Your website is your opportunity to sell yourself immediately before a potential client picks up the phone to you. Getting it right will add a huge amount of value to your sales process. If, however, you make it difficult to find out what you do and how you work, or whether you're right for them, you'll likely never have that phone call as they'll give up and work with someone else.

Working with a designer

There are plenty of brilliant web designers who will professionally design and build a website that is perfect for your business, that speaks to your audience and that means you can be found.

The benefits of working with a professional website designer are:

* They will build a website that works with your business branding
* They are experienced at building websites that sell and will write your webpages for you
* They will be able to help you get found by optimising your website for search engines. This is known as Search Engine Optimisation.
* And of course, you won't need to build your own website!

We're just going to leave this with you for a moment.

We suspect many of your potential clients come to you having completed their own bookkeeping in the past. If you're like many of the bookkeepers in our community, you'll sometimes worry that convincing your clients to outsource the work to you is going to be a hard sell. But you know deep down that it is right for the client to outsource the work to you, an expert, because that will give them the time back in their business to focus on what generates income for them.

It's the same for you.

In the next sections, we'll explain how you can build your own website. It's important to remember that if you get trapped in the cycle of doing everything for your business yourself, you'll never start or grow your business.

Do what is necessary.

> Outsource those things you're not an expert in.

Just as you'd say to your clients.

Building your own website

For most new bookkeepers, working with a professional designer is out of the question for budget reasons, and you might decide to have a go at building your own website (or ask a competent friend or family member to help) using one of the many online website building tools.

Some suggestions to get you started are Wix, Wordpress and Squarespace. Each works in a very similar way, allowing you to find and customise a template that works for you so you can get a website online within a few hours.

Customisable templates are available, which you can adapt to include details about who you help, your services, and where potential clients can even book a call with you online. Your website can manage an email list and even support you with scheduling and showcasing your social media content.

Let them know they're in the right place

A website doesn't need to be complicated. It's your way to show your ideal client that they're in the right place and that you're the bookkeeper for them. And ultimately to help them take action and book a call with you.

How do you help them know they're in the right place so they're encouraged to book that call? You speak their language through your words and your brand. You show that you have the knowledge, experience and credibility to solve their problem.

We recommend that you don't list every single method of contacting you – clients need solutions fast, so give your website visitors one action – a button to book a call.

> We don't want to overcomplicate this because websites are one of the biggest barriers bookkeepers have to getting their businesses started. Just get it out there.

A word of warning. We go back to the point that when you don't need to, you would be wise to outsource a task like this. Your website is your shop window online so remember its purpose. This is the first impression you're going to give a potential client.

A poor website won't convert leads into clients – visitors will simply leave. The return on investment of getting this right can be huge.

Social media

So you have a lovely website and once your name is typed into a search bar your client will be taken to it. There's even a button taking them to your calendar to book a meeting. But if they don't know who you are yet, how else can your new clients find you?

Social media plays an important role here. Some people actually won't type your name into a search engine, they might type it into their favourite social media app. Or they might type "bookkeeper". Or "accountant". Or something related to the problem they have.

It's easy to become overwhelmed with the number of social media platforms we think we "should" be using. And they can become a huge distraction from what we need to be doing day to day to move our businesses forward.

Our advice is simple. We need to spend our time where our ideal client is. If they're on LinkedIn, that's where we need to be. If they're on Facebook, we need to think about setting up a Facebook page or a group, or joining the groups they're a part of. If they're on TikTok, then we're sorry to say it, but you're going to need to be on TikTok.

People are addicted to their phones, and one of our favourite ever anecdotes from an episode of The Bookkeepers' Podcast was when we were told that someone's favourite social media app is the one they open in the bathroom! Your ideal clients need to see you there, consistently, showing up and proving that you're the best person to solve their problems.

They might not be ready to have their problems solved today, but when that brown envelope lands on the doormat from HMRC, you'll be front of mind as the person to call.

A social media strategy is important for your business, so as you start and build your business, as you seek more leads, think about what your ideal client needs to hear from you to show them that you are an authority in this area.

We recommend that no matter where you are posting, you share a style of content that you're most comfortable with and that your ideal client will relate to. Our experience is that at the time of writing, short videos (reels and TikToks) get the best reach, and if you're good on camera, this can be a great way of connecting with your ideal client. If you're more about writing, consider a blog – which would also be great longform content for your website – broken down into longform text posts or shorter "top tips"-style grid posts for Instagram, which can be used over a series of days.

Your content can cycle between sharing your knowledge, sharing details of your experience, showing you understand their industry, and helping people get to know you. Covering these four aspects will help you become trusted as the best-placed bookkeeper to support your ideal client in their business.

There are so many options, and this is why bookkeepers in our world often find social media to be overwhelming. Just take it back to you and your clients. What do you enjoy? What do they need to see? How can you bring your two worlds together in the most effective way?

And always remember your call to action.

Always tell your potential client what to do next – to book a call with you.

Summary

In this section we have considered the two main elements of marketing your business online: social media and your website. Marketing is important, and in this virtual world we need to pay attention to where our clients are and be there as well. Marketing keeps so many people stuck, and this can be one of the best tasks to outsource, particularly if you don't see yourself as creative or inspired in this area.

We have, however, seen some incredible online marketing by bookkeepers who've really got this right. From brightly coloured websites to YouTube channels, you really can take this wherever you want to if you're inspired and have the skills and desire.

So go back to Chapter 2, think again about your ideal client, and then create a plan for the quarter and wholeheartedly commit to doing one thing well. Oh and connect with us so we can see what you're working on (you'll find us on Facebook, Instagram, LinkedIn and even TikTok).

Chapter 7

YOUR PERSONAL BRAND

We've spent a lot of time talking about your business and how it will show up online. But what about you? Another stumbling block for bookkeepers and something that you might be stuck with too is the idea of raising your own profile.

We think this happens because we're not used to it being OK to draw attention to ourselves. We don't like putting ourselves out there and saying "Hey! I'm here! It's me!" in case we're judged or in case somebody doesn't like us.

> But getting visible is critical if you're going to grow your business.

So far in this book, you've considered four steps of the framework that we teach bookkeepers so they can start and scale bookkeeping practices.

You've become aware of the mindset that might be holding you back. You've thought about your ideal client in detail, you've considered the services you will offer them, and you've considered how you will make sure they know about your business and that it's the right business to serve their needs.

We'll come onto the systems that allow you to deliver those services in the next section. Now, though, it's time for you to get yourself out there.

We want you to find clients. You need to start bringing them into your business so you need to consider a marketing plan not just for the business but also for making sure that you, the business owner, are visible. This isn't to say you need to do all of the work, but being a known figure, a credible expert, will drive business to you.

> We believe that the best way to connect with an ideal client is not to plonk a great looking business in front of them that solves their problems, but to put a person in front of them who has the answers to their problems.

Hopefully you now have an idea of how much you want to earn, how many clients you need, and how much you need your clients to pay you to achieve your goals. Once you can see that, and you have a plan for how much you want to grow by each month, we can put in place a plan and start to implement what needs to be done to start those sales calls.

It can feel very difficult to get over feelings of imposter syndrome and become more visible, but you need to come at this challenge by thinking of the value you're giving to people so they have a better experience in business. Be your genuine self and give value and it will be difficult to go wrong.

Where you choose to build your personal brand will come down to what's right for you and where you need to be seen by your ideal client. Wherever you choose to be, start tracking your numbers.

We, for example, track our connections on Facebook, LinkedIn and on YouTube,as well as our podcast listens. Then we get into detail of where those connections and listeners are based and how they come into our world. The same applies for you in your practice.

We recommend that you look for opportunities to show your credibility and authority and to help people get to know you as a normal human being! This usually looks like a combination of:

* Articles, posts or videos on social media that demonstrate that you know your field
* Posts that show what you do in business
* Posts that celebrate your clients – with a secondary motive of showing you have clients like your ideal client
* And finally posts that show that you're a decent person who your ideal client would like to do business with

Maybe you feel you have enough on your plate already by creating social media content for your business accounts, and you don't have to start separate accounts if you don't want to. Simply show up as yourself on your business accounts. Post videos with you speaking and share photos of yourself doing what you do.

We know that the idea of planning posts for social media can feel incredibly overwhelming, so don't overthink it. Make a commitment to show up on one platform two or three times per week. Decide what you're going to do and put it in your diary. Once you've got into the habit, it becomes easier.

We've worked hard on our personal brands over the two years that have led to writing this book, and we believe that focusing on our ideal client, helping people get to know us, and being consistent has paid off. We've been able to become known for speaking about particular topics and that's led to opportunities to present webinars, to join podcasts, to write articles and to collaborate with various social media influencers who also work in our space.

Sometimes you have to ask for the opportunity as well – particularly as you start to build your brand. We've not been shy about asking for opportunities when we've known we can add value.

We believe we make our own futures, and building a strong personal brand that gets you known by your ideal client is one of the quickest routes to being seen as a valuable expert.

Summary

In this chapter, we've considered the importance of your personal brand within your business. Showing up is one of the biggest challenges for bookkeepers – we're not used to being the centre of attention, we usually identify with being introverts, and when we're changing profession or becoming self-employed for the first time, it can feel paralysing to think about starting to raise your profile when people you know from old jobs are just waiting for you to slip up and fail. But they're not. And we have to know that if we're going to build the businesses we want for the future, we need to take the actions that get us ready for that future, and that starts with a little self-belief.

SYSTEMS FOR GROWTH

Version one is better than version zero.

~ Chris Johnson

Chapter 8

OPERATIONS AND APPS

Jo: My mum made me read The E Myth by Michael E. Gerber when I first started my bookkeeping business back in 2003. Later, when I went into partnership with a large accountancy firm, I learned that every member of their staff had their own copy. This impressed me, and knowing how important the core message of the book was, I did the same with my own staff.

What I've learnt from The E Myth, and what I know to be true from years in the industry, is this: People know how to do a job. And people believe that because they can do that job, they could run a business better than their boss.

Have you ever been in that situation? Have you ever thought, "I'm really good at this, I could do this my own way by my own rules"? After all, people paid your employer – why wouldn't they pay you? You might even have thought that without the overheads you could do it cheaper as well!

This is common for bookkeepers starting practices. Often bookkeepers are looking for a more flexible way of working that they can't get from employment so they start out on their own.

From experiences in employment, they have ideas about how they'd do things differently. And this is the entrepreneurial myth. We believe that as technicians, we understand how to do a task and so we believe we understand how to run a better business. But running a business has so much more to it.

There's an operational part to a business – the service that your client pays for – but when we start out, we often overlook the other aspects involved in running a business.

Business ownership is also about sales, HR, contracts, marketing and so much more. Entrepreneurs tend to go into business knowing the operational part of what they're going to do, but without having mastered the craft of running a business, many of them fail.

So far in this book, we've taught you four of the five steps of our framework for finding clients. What we need to do now, is build systems which deliver a great service, efficiently, without us burning out.

In this section we'll talk about systems, we'll challenge you to consider yourself as a business owner. You are the person who can have the vision and who can put the structure in place. You don't need to be the doer of all things, and if you know that from the start, you are much more likely to achieve success.

McDonald's is a business run by teenagers because they've got their systems down, and that's what we need to do. McDonald's staff are told exactly how many seconds to cook the burger for, and each slice of cheese is a standard size and weight. The staff know that you put the burger there, you put a little bit of sauce there, and you put the gherkin on top. There are pictures for them to look at so that they know how to do it and what it should look like. There are buzzers that go off and tell them what to do and when. And you might well be shaking your head right now, thinking that is not the way you want to do the bookkeeping. But our point is that when you systemise, you don't need to do the bookkeeping – you can become the business owner, you can do the things that make a difference and grow your business. You add the value and build a business you want to run, rather than becoming a repeater of processes.

Standardising processes

There are a lot of processes in our business that we don't even see as processes, and the first step in standardising any process is becoming aware of repetition. Repetitive tasks are the first things you can remove yourself from as you can systemise them, document them and outsource or delegate them. It's great to start when you're less busy as even if you have no one to hand that process over to right now, you'll notice if you have any inefficiencies or inconsistency, and you will find much needed headspace to have a process or checklist to work to.

We all have our own preferences as to how we do this, and you'll have yours. Think of this as a project of creating a directory of processes. It sounds big, but we promise that the sooner you start, the sooner you will reach the end. What's critical is finding your preferred way to ensure you can stick it out because it will pay off.

Zoe: We recently sat down and mapped out the processes we follow to market and run a virtual event in our Facebook group. It's a free week-long event we run to inspire and support our bookkeeping community. We found that there are 94 unique steps, and some of those steps are repeated multiple times.

A great way to start the task of systemising your business is to simply brainstorm every task you can think of, grouping them into categories where applicable.

The category of onboarding, for example, might include: sending a welcome email to your client, inviting them to an onboarding meeting, requesting their ID, logging into their accounting software, inviting your client to your receipt capture software, setting up invoicing and so on – provided, of course, that none of these tasks are already automated.

Jo: One of the biggest processes that I have been able to outsource has been email management. We tend to do this ourselves because we don't want someone touching our inboxes. But actually, when I created a process around this and really spoke to a virtual assistant about it, it saved me so much time. I believe it's about trust, and it's easier to have trust when you deliberately decide how a system or process should look.

Systems allow us to start seeing where we're really effective and the processes we're really good at are in fact the ones we can outsource fastest because we know all of the steps and we know exactly what success looks like for somebody who's following that process.

A question we must ask at this point is where do you bring the most value in your business? We don't think it will be with you reconciling each and every bank line.

How to get started

Often we speak to bookkeepers who are desperate to remove themselves from their businesses, to bring in support, and to get away from the client work, but they're completely overwhelmed by their workload. The idea of documenting anything or delegating and training somebody up is too much given the time pressure they're already under. They'd rather work some extra hours to get the work done themselves, because surely at some point it will get easier...

We know there are busy periods but if you don't want to burn out, here's how we suggest you get started with systems so you can automate and delegate in the least overwhelming way.

Grab some paper, or start a spreadsheet if you like, and along the top write the core activities in your business. Your list will include client work – maybe split into different types of activity depending on your core services. Also include sales and marketing activity, onboarding, AML, administration, and email management.

Now brainstorm absolutely every activity involved under each heading. Marketing, for example, might involve a monthly content planning session, creating images for different platforms, pre-writing three posts for each week, recording four videos, creating a YouTube thumbnail for each, writing a caption, researching networking events for the month ahead, connecting with everyone on LinkedIn that attends the event, and so on.

These are just top line tasks, but once you have these headers, the next time you complete that task – because these things are repetitive and can follow a process even when we tell ourselves they can't – we can document every single step involved. Either on paper, on a spreadsheet, or even on video, so next time someone else can pick up the process.

This is fundamental for you to scale and bring in support.

Zoe: *Something that's worked really well for me is to film processes. There's no end of tools that allow you to record your screen and share your processes. I like to hit record and go through the process as I normally would, just making sure I explain each step in detail. I then file videos using the naming conventions that make sense for the business. Sometimes I even watch them back myself!*

Obviously these videos don't include any passwords, which are saved securely, and it's important to make sure there's information about why this process is important, who it applies to, where it fits in to the business in general, and the precise deliverables and timeframes. It can be helpful to have a supplementary checklist running alongside if this isn't already held inside your practice management system.

Growing through technology

Apps and software are incredibly effective in helping you automate your business systems and leverage your time so you can concentrate on building your business rather than doing the bookkeeping. These tools have been designed to save you time and money, and we should consider them to be our first investment in growing our businesses because some of the great apps out there are as effective as having another team member.

A word of caution. It is easy to get waylaid when faced with the next shiny object – or app. Our advice is to focus on one part of your business, consider other systems you already have or plan to have, and choose the app that will integrate the best, create the workflow you want, and improve that area of your business.

Jo: When I launched Jo Wood Virtual FD I had just a handful of apps. And I started by choosing an accounting software and a data extraction tool.

It might seem like an investment when you haven't even got a client, but we shouldn't be keying everything in ourselves. There's so much time saved when you consider the role of software in leveraging your time rather than seeing it as a 'cost'.

Our advice is to choose software that is good for you and also for your clients, so there is no one-size-fits-all solution that we can recommend. Most software will, however, give you a free trial, training and an account manager who can train you and guide you through getting the most out of it, so ask them for help.

Once you have those fundamental software solutions bedded in, you might then look to partner with other tools that support you and your clients with everything from cash flow forecasting to reporting, to credit control and applying for funding. The mix that is right for you and your clients will be determined by the challenges your ideal client faces. This is why we emphasise niching so much, because it makes all of these decisions easier as you build your business.

Jo: I like to think of my software account managers as part of my management team. I check in with them once a month to see how I'm using that software. If I'm not using it to the best of its ability, then there are efficiencies that can be made.

You can't be everything to everyone

It's easy to become overwhelmed when it comes to software, and we need to bring you back to your ideal client here.

You can't be the expert in everything. And why would you try to be?

We believe we can run the best businesses that are most valuable to our clients when we get really good at one thing.

And the best way to specialise is to have a process – a clear way of working that you follow. This helps your clients know what to expect; it helps you know what you are delivering, and it means you can bring other people into your business so they can run those processes for you, rather than everything falling to you.

The best business is a profitable business that works without us. So when a business depends on us to do everything, we really don't have a business. We certainly don't have anything scalable.

Zoe: *I had an intern who worked seven hours a week around her uni schedule. Trying to teach her three different pieces of software would have been an inefficient use of my time. I needed her to learn processes that all used the same software to help her be the most productive. The best way to do that was to allocate her work that looked the same, but for different clients. She only had to learn the software once. She only had to learn the process once.*

It's the same for us. It's easy to think we should know an extra piece of software "just in case". But the truth is that we can get distracted by doing all of the advisor certifications or speaking to our account managers, whereas we can leverage our time best when we become absolute experts at just one piece of software or a small selection of different software solutions that complement each other.

Which other tools will I need?

You'll likely bring in other tools to support you with the services you provide, whether those are tools to support you in preparing a proposal, with management information, dedicated payroll software or credit control tools. When you know the challenges of your ideal client and when you map out the service they really need to hit their goals and solve their problems, you'll know whether a piece of software is really needed or the right fit.

We also advise using some form of Customer Relationship Management tool or CRM. Accountancy-specific CRMs will also manage your workflows, store files, integrate with other software in the industry, and even manage your email marketing sequences. You'll know from this book so far that we're all about challenging you to think bigger than where your business is today, and to build the business you're aiming for in the future, you need the right tools now. A practice management tool or CRM will give you confidence and control as you grow.

Diary management is the bane of every small business owner's life. And something that will save you time before you even consider hiring an assistant or admin support is a few automations around your diary. There are plenty of scheduling tools you can register with that will allow potential clients to choose a time that suits them from your diary, fill in a form with some details, and even receive automated text reminders before your meeting. This has the added benefit of you being able to predefine which days and times you actually want to be available. Spend half an hour setting this up before you even have your first enquiry, share your booking link as your call to action in every piece of marketing you do, and thank us later.

In this virtual world, video is the final essential tool we'll discuss in this section. We believe you will need a way to create video and communicate by video – it's an essential tool right now for any business owner.

You'll probably use it to meet with clients, to communicate with them, train them, and also to document processes in your business. Don't overlook the value of video as there are opportunities to use it throughout your business.

Summary

In this chapter, we've considered how important it is to have systems that can allow your business to grow. It's so tempting when we start in business to do all the things, to bootstrap, to put up with a bit of extra data entry or a few slightly annoying workarounds because it's just us and it saves us a bit of money.

But one day, these things will be frustrating. One day, you'll be at capacity but too busy with your workarounds to find the time to hire staff, or you won't have time for a sales call because you're too busy doing your client work because it isn't streamlined, meaning you'll lose a sale.

Systemising your business, bringing in automations and using tech that helps you leverage your time will mean you can focus on what's really important – growing your business.

Chapter 9
STAFFING

Deciding whether and when to bring people into their team is one of the hardest decisions for many of the bookkeepers in our community.

When you start your business, you start as you. You do the work, you do the sales calls, you send the proposal, you do everything. The opportunity to only answer to yourself might have been the reason you started your bookkeeping business in the first place.

But at some point you'll be busy, or you'll see that you could bring more money into the business if you had an extra pair of hands. The responsibility that comes with having a team, however, can feel terrifying.

This chapter is about when to make the decision to bring in staffing, and what you need to consider as you scale your practice through people.

You might be thinking "I never want to scale, this chapter isn't for me" and be tempted to skip ahead. But trust us that when your business can run without you, that's when you'll be truly successful in your business. There's also bound to be a day you need a holiday or a sick day and you don't want to be worrying about your emails or your client work, so let's start thinking about this now as we build your business ready for the future.

> *Jo:* I have had a rough time employing staff. But I've now learnt that that was sometimes my fault. It was my fault because I didn't always recruit very well. Sometimes we get so, so busy that I'd think 'Oh, I just wish someone would come in and do this and do that and take it away.' But what we've got to realise is that we need to be outsourcing or employing before that point, and we need to be doing it when we have some time to give to that person. It's really unfair to bring people into your business and not give them the support they need to succeed."

Your pricing is key

One of the biggest resistances we get to bringing in support either from staff or subcontractors is that 'there won't be any money left for me'. If this is the case, you have a pricing problem.

Why are you running your business? We believe you run your business to make a profit, and there should always be a margin on your work that rewards you, the business owner, regardless of whether you do the actual work. That margin is higher than you might think, and if you're feeling resistant or that you don't think you can "charge that much", this is something you must revisit. Unless you reconsider your pricing right now, you're going to face a challenge.

Employee or contractor

If you're worried about whether you can afford to bring in staff, you'll probably be wondering how much it will cost to bring somebody into your team. Particularly if you've never considered being an employer before.

This is going to depend on who you need. And our first suggestion is that you look at your business, your clients and where your time is best used, and identify who would be right to bring in to support different areas of the business.

You won't just need bookkeeping support – in fact, administrative support might be one of the first roles you need to fill, but for the purposes of this next section we'll assume you need more bookkeepers.

The systems you have in your business will determine what level of support you need and which skills your team needs. If you have a heavily systemised business and the support you need is likely to be at a junior level, you may be able to bring somebody in at quite a low hourly rate, but if they're less experienced and potentially less emotionally mature, be prepared to give them more support than somebody more senior.

A more experienced and senior member of staff might be able to help you with more technical work – supporting junior team members and looking after or even setting up automations and systems – at a higher salary, but with potentially less demand on your time.

Either way, in the UK, we'd say that bringing in an employee on payroll will probably cost your business less on an hourly rate basis than bringing in a subcontractor – who will likely charge more due to the risk they take by being self employed.

There are other factors to consider, however, when it comes to the cost and risk of taking on an employee. These include your responsibility to look after their health and safety at work, ensuring you have the correct legal policies and insurances in place to protect your employee and your business. You will probably need to provide a pension, sick pay, holiday, equipment and potentially office space and other support.

One option some practices consider as they test out their need for staff is to take on contractors. The benefits are that your contractors may be able to work from home or their own offices, which is great if you work virtually. They will likely have more experience of working for other practices and clients and they'll have their own equipment and their own insurance. They give you the flexibility to increase or reduce the hours you need based on your workload.

One of the biggest challenges we discuss with bookkeepers is the timings around scaling. How close to capacity do you let yourself get before you bring staff in? How much should they be contributing to business turnover? We think the key factors here are your goals and your pricing.

We're going to be honest with you here. If your pricing is right, your turnover when you're at full capacity will more than cover the cost of bringing an employee into the business at the level you need to replace yourself. So if your pipeline is filled with new leads and you're keeping your foot on the gas having sales conversations and onboarding new clients, you can bring somebody new into the business before you need them. You'll have time to train them and can turn your attention to sales calls to bring them up to capacity.

The problem is that most bookkeepers don't have this foresight and reach capacity before they think about bringing in extra team members. That means by the time they think about hiring (and remember there could be several months before you find the right person and actually onboard them), they're already stretched and actually afraid to take sales calls in case they get another client! They take their foot off the gas, they stop marketing, stop getting leads, and wonder how they'll ever be able to get all of their work done and market and hire staff – and afford it all.

Our recommendation is to get your pricing right, find the balance of marketing that works for you and hire your first team member before you're at capacity.

> Your job as a business owner isn't to do the day to day work. It's to drive the business forward. And if you only do the bookkeeping, you'll never be able to step into that role.

Zoe: "My first team member was a subcontractor. I didn't want to get involved in payroll so I brought somebody in who offered this service. She then started to work some hours every month for a few of my clients so I could test out my need for my first employee. When I was pregnant I knew I wouldn't be able to work in the business all the time, and that trial of subcontracting gave me confidence to bring in my first employees. My team meant I could remove myself from the day-to-day business activities and take care of my son while still being paid."

Hiring

The exercise above might have opened your eyes to a need within your business for more support. And you may have a preference for whether this is a permanent employee or a subcontractor.

The next step is to find that person.

Being clear from the outset on the roles and responsibilities that make up that position is important, otherwise how can we measure the success of that person? And they will want to know too. They will want to know what's expected of them so they can feel they're hitting targets and performing.

Start with an organisation structure. Which teams do you need in your business for it to hit the goals you have for it? And which people will fill those teams?

Right now, you are heading up each team, and you are probably doing the role of every person in every team, so the next step is to consider where your time is best spent to add value to the business, and which gaps that leaves.

This work and your understanding of business systems from Chapter 8 will be the foundations of your new hire's job description. The job description is a list of what is involved in the role and its areas of responsibility, as well as the key tasks that make up the position.

We also recommend that you develop a person specification for the role. There may be qualifications and certifications you need for the role or you might be looking for somebody with a certain amount of experience or experience in a particular sector or industry. You can develop your person specification even further by thinking about the personality of the person you want to bring into the team.

Think of this as the kind of exercise you might do with your ideal client. What is your ideal employee like as a person? What motivates them? What do they bring to the team? What do they love to do? Thinking through this information will make your selection process much more straightforward because you can eliminate those who don't fit the bill and score candidates against your list of requirements.

Personality fit is so important but often overlooked, especially when you have a small team. In a team, you have all sorts of different personalities. Every new person can change a team dynamic, and you'll find that people take different roles as the team establishes itself.

You have to work with these people every day, and you might also want to put them in front of your clients. The team you bring in reflects your business and your business's reputation.

Where to advertise

Where you choose to advertise will come down to where you want to be seen and where your ideal candidate is likely to be looking.

Most bookkeepers don't choose to use a recruiter and you'll probably decide to manage the recruitment process yourself. If you're looking for somebody local to you, you might choose to advertise on local jobs boards or even at colleges depending on the level you're recruiting at. There are many free jobs websites with freemium upgrade options, and then you have LinkedIn, your website and your own social media profiles. If you're a member of a professional body you might also be able to advertise on its jobs board.

We recommend that you make an ad short and succinct, outlining what you're looking for and clearly stating what you need to receive from the candidate to consider their application. We think a covering letter can go a long way in helping to assess how well the candidate has researched you and actually wants the job. Some jobs websites will also allow you to set a test for the candidate on a skill such as Excel or numeracy.

If you specifically request a cover letter and the candidate fails to include one, you should ask whether they're going to have good enough attention to detail for you when it comes to the day-to-day role.

Zoe: *The best hire I've made so far was, believe it or not, through Instagram. I hired somebody who was already following my business and knew what we did. This gave her an instant head start over anyone I could have found through a listing on a directory. She knew what we were about and she even knew some of our client base. It helped so much.*

We recommend that you score your applicants against a framework. This will allow you to choose the top applicants for interview, particularly if you receive a lot of applications.

To save time, you could also set up a 15-minute chat before the formal interview round to narrow your list down further. We're all short of time, and when diaries are tricky, the last thing you want is to set two days aside for interviews over the next fortnight and still potentially not have made a decision.

During these short interviews you can simply ask candidates what they know about your business and why they want the job. Without doubt, this is going to show who has done their homework, who has not, and who is invested in the application process.

Onboarding

Whether you hire full-time employees, part-time employees, or subcontractors, they all need to be made to feel part of your team. Your onboarding process will set the scene for how you work together and build your relationship.

We've both experienced some terrible onboarding and induction processes in our time, and our learnings from having to set up our own computers, spending hours on hold to IT before we could log in to the network, has taught us that we want our team members to feel welcomed, supported and productive straight away. This doesn't happen by chance, so we need to think about onboarding even before our new hire's first day. The foundations you build with somebody new to your business set the scene for the culture of your business.

Think about whether you could drop your new team member an email before they start work to let them know you're looking forward to welcoming them. Tell them where to be and when, and mention who they will be speaking to.

Then make a plan to welcome them into the business. Share some of the story behind your business, share your values, and help them get to know a bit about some of your clients before giving them some work to do to help them feel productive – and to give you a break! First days are hard for both employees and employers, so take the time to plan it out.

Also, expect a new team member to change the dynamic within your existing team. Your usual flow will be disrupted and some team members may feel threatened, so be prepared to put everyone at ease.

Managing your team

When you're at capacity and your new team member has finally arrived, it's tempting to breathe a sigh of relief and let them get on with it.

But just like everything we've said so far in this book, we want to build businesses that are set up for the future. That means stepping into our roles as leaders so we can build a motivated team and get value from our staff.

See it from your new team member's perspective. There's nothing worse than having a pile of work dumped on you. It's equally frustrating when you work for someone who checks in with you every two minutes. Both might be tempting at the beginning, so we need to maintain control through a good reporting process.

Systems and processes are the way to know that you're in control, so go back to the systems for your client work and make sure you've documented the steps that need to be followed. Design checklists and sign-off processes that ensure you have confidence the work is being done to the standard you expect, and that hold your employees accountable.

However competent your team members, your staff also need to know when they need to escalate things to you. You want to feel that everything's in hand, but you don't want to do everything yourself, so you need to be able to trust that your team knows when to reach out. Many bookkeepers find it very difficult to delegate and hand work over, so having a process you're comfortable with will give you confidence as you reach this level.

Jo: I have the same process for each client. When I brought a new team member in recently, I got her started with items one, two, and three on the checklist first for multiple clients. Then I reviewed them. Once she was getting those all correct and I had no review points or queries for her at any of those steps, I let her do four and five. Now she's right down to the bottom of the list. This might be a slower process than you'd expect, but I got confidence from those first few tasks across multiple clients. She wanted to have more responsibility, so she was motivated to learn our way of doing things.

You might decide not to use manual checklists but to build workflows and sign-offs into a piece of practice management software or a project management tool that will allow you at a glance to see what's due and let you allocate work to different people, keeping notes and files and communicating within the team.

Having a review process in place helps you train your staff in your expectations, as does having weekly team meetings or check-ins. These are especially important in this world where we work virtually and it's easy to miss when somebody is struggling.

It's helpful to keep these meetings to a set agenda to stay on track and ensure your team know what they're going to be asked, as well as to feel assured that they'll have an opportunity to ask for support where they need it.

Ultimately, we want you to be in a position where you don't need to firefight. If you have loads of staff, loads of clients and no systems or reporting processes, you'll find yourself constantly putting out fires or dealing with problems. Nobody wants that. Use your team meeting agendas and checklists as opportunities to ensure that every single fire is addressed and in some way avoided for future. Maybe that's because of a new agenda item or a new checkbox on the list. Always think about the future, because putting in the work now is how you will build the business that supports your future success.

Summary

There's a lot to consider when it comes to growing a team, and many bookkeepers we work with are adamant that it will only ever be them in their business. But we know that if you open your mind to the idea that you will at some point need support and that support is a good thing for your business as opposed to a cost, you will be able to set your business up for success and growth.

Chapter 10

A BOOKKEEPING BUSINESS WITH STRATEGY

Building a bookkeeping business with an intentional strategy to achieve your goals gives you the best chance of success.

Some time ago, a bookkeeper posted in our free group, The 6 Figure Bookkeepers' Club, that she'd hit six figures in turnover. We celebrated her success with huge congratulations, comments and well wishes. One of the comments asked her what she had found the most helpful from what she'd learnt on The Bookkeepers' 6 Month Success Programme – our programme for bookkeepers – and she commented that she wasn't a member of the programme. It had taken years for her to find her way, but she'd finally hit her goal.

Contrast this with Annabel, a bookkeeper who's worked with us over the last year or so to build her practice. Eleven months ago, she incorporated her limited company, and this week she told us she'd hit six figures.

She got there through vision, hard work and commitment - just like the other bookkeeper in our community. But working with others who are on a similar path, benefiting from the collective knowledge of others and having the support of an ambitious, like-minded community of business owners accelerated her success.

We've been told all sorts of statistics as we've started and grown our own businesses, maybe you have too.

We've been told:

* You can't expect to make a profit until year three
* 80% of businesses fail within five years
* One in five businesses fail every year

And whether those statistics are true or not, they are powerful and can lead you to doubt yourself. These are the kinds of stats that loved ones might say to you, not because they don't believe in you, but because they want to protect you from failure.

That's why you need ambitious people to support you in this journey, and we've built a community of like-minded bookkeepers who want to share the route to success so you don't have to spend years figuring it all out for yourself. We've built a training programme in which we share what we've learnt in business, where you can learn from Jo as she shares how she's reached multiple six figures and how she's been able to build a business that supports her family - and even employs some of her family members - while she works just school hours.

We know that building a strategy that leverages learnings from others who've trodden the path you're on right now will fast-track you to where you want to be.

The no-strategy risk

Jo: "I've run several bookkeeping practices. Not all of them were a success for various reasons, and I've been on a huge journey of learning and personal development. When I started Jo Wood Virtual FD in 2019 I made a commitment to myself that this was my final practice. I was going to hit six figures. And I made such a commitment to myself that I set up a Facebook group and called it The 6 Figure Bookkeepers' Club. This time was different and I was going to have a strategy, and I wrote down step by step exactly what I was going to do to hit my goals.

"I made a commitment to get the right software, the right systems, and the right support."

We have mentioned several times throughout this book how, when we start our businesses, we don't often see them as businesses. We become absorbed in the process of doing brilliant bookkeeping, and the risk to all business owners is that they become absorbed in the operations, creating a job for themselves rather than a profitable business.

It makes sense. Many of us join this profession from a background of employment, sometimes from financial and administrative backgrounds, but often from entirely different professions. We are unlikely to know what is involved in growing a business, let alone reaching financial goals that potentially stretch far beyond what we've ever earned in employment. There's no shame in not knowing.

But we are business owners. And we challenge you, through everything you've read so far in this book, to know that your business can achieve greater success than you might have originally thought.

Community

The lack of business knowledge is the reason building a community of like-minded bookkeepers has been so important to us. Of course we know a lot about building six figure businesses, but the power is also in the wealth of what is known within our community. Imagine jumping into a group of 100 or more bookkeeping and accounting professionals who are all building their own businesses, where you can ask any question that's on your mind and likely find somebody who's experienced exactly the same thing and already has the answer.

We know that you can find the answers and you can build your business. But how quickly can you get there on your own?

Maybe you'll hit six figures in ten years' time. But where could you be in ten years' time if you leveraged the knowledge of a community who've already answered a lot of your questions? What if, like Jo, you could reach six figures in two years? What would year ten look like for you then?

We've both spent a lot of time and money on coaching and mentoring in business. We've paid for everything from sales training to mindset coaching. We've had marketing training and life coaching. We've been on training about how to build memberships and courses and we've had legal training. Zoe's even been trained in neuro-linguistic programming. We've been coached one-to-one and we've joined group programmes and masterminds – some of them virtual, some of them in person. Jo even spent a few days in Spain with one of her coaches. At the time of writing, we're working with at least three coaches and mentors between us, and we believe that coaching and business development is an essential ongoing process for us as business owners.

We believe in developing ourselves so we can be better versions of ourselves. And because we serve a community, we also know that through our learnings we can inspire others who haven't yet discovered the power of bringing that guidance and support into their lives and businesses.

Why are we telling you this?

At the start of our business, we never thought of having a coach. We decided coaching was expensive and because we would rather work things out for ourselves, we didn't see the value in it. We thought we could search online for any information we would need about growing a business anyway, and were quite fearful of spending money when there were plenty of practical things like software that needed our money instead.

But it became clear when we had conversations with people who were one or two steps ahead that what they knew was invaluable for us. Then we started to see the value of leveraging their knowledge to create quicker learnings for ourselves, and more income for ourselves. Rather than thinking about what it would cost us to spend on coaching, we saw what we were able to earn if we made an investment in coaching. It was a change of mindset.

The knowledge and insight we were gaining felt like an acceleration that allowed us to become more decisive and take action. And this affected every part of our business. It might be being able to choose a piece of software because we knew the advantages of it over something else for our specific way of working or our specific client base. It could be knowing what to say to a disorganised client so they'd see the value of cooperating and providing the paperwork we needed so we didn't need to work the weekend. Or it could be knowing how to hold a sales call confidently because the people we were speaking to had sales calls every single day.

What's next for you

Throughout this book, we've aimed to share what we think every bookkeeper needs to know to launch and grow a bookkeeping business that serves their needs and helps them achieve their goals. We never could have fitted everything we know into a book, and as we learn and grow as business owners ourselves, we think this is a book we could rewrite year-in, year-out.

What we hope you've left with is a guide to the key areas we know you must consider, guided by our 5-step Framework:

* Reset – focusing on your goals
* Ideal client – so you know who you're trying to reach
* Service – so what you sell is aligned with who you want to serve

* Engage – so you can become known by the market you want to connect with
* Systems - streamlining and organising your business with processes and people.

But what's next?

If you've read this book and taken action, you'll be feeling positive and energised about what is to come. But maybe you need more support. We support bookkeepers in many ways, through our free 6 Figure Bookkeepers' Club on Facebook, which you're welcome to join, and through our 6 Month Success Programme designed for bookkeepers working on the various issues we have covered in this book.

And if you'd like the support of like-minded bookkeepers around you as you take your next steps, we'd love to talk to you about how we could support you in your business. You can book a free, no obligation discovery call with us here: **6figurebookkeeper.com/call** - *or scan the handy QR below.*

Part 2

Inspirational Stories

Stories

We work with an incredible community of bookkeepers and accountants, and in this next section we want to share with you the huge range of reasons people start bookkeeping businesses, and the possibilities that those businesses create for balance, income and family life.

We are sure there will be somebody within this section of the book that you connect with and are inspired by.

Luna Ballard - Lava Sky Accounting

When I'm not working, my free time is dedicated to triathlon – a sport my husband and I are passionate about. We pass the hours swimming, cycling or running for health, fitness and mental wellbeing. We love to challenge ourselves and have adventures. In the past, this has meant competing in Ironman triathlons, ultramarathons and a cycle tour around New Zealand. Other times things are a little more relaxed: a long ride or run on a sunny day – with a cake stop, of course!

Following my undergraduate and masters degrees in sport and health, I set up my own personal training and triathlon coaching business. As a fitness enthusiast, I loved passing on my love of movement and exercise to others, helping them achieve their goals – no matter how big or small – and supporting them to make healthy lifestyle choices. However, I found what I really enjoyed was the financial side of running a business. I wanted to learn more, so I took a bookkeeping course. I soon realised that not only did I have a natural affinity for it, I also had fun in the process. It was the first time it felt cool to be a geek!

That's when I decided to switch career paths from fitness to finance. Saving the former as my passion and outlet, while using the other to develop my working life.

Before long, I found myself leading the finances for a small company whilst studying for my accountancy qualification. I also doubled down by training for an Ironman at the same time! I spent over 10 years working in finance. During this time, I was very fortunate to work with great financial directors who taught me so much. I also worked for several companies that had lots of different sectors within them. This meant I got to experience a wide range of industries including leisure, hospitality, retail, recruitment and banking.

Through all that, it was always a goal in the back of my mind to get back to the grassroots of accounting and run my own business again. One of the things that attracted me to sports coaching was supporting people and I realised this could be re-applied with my experience in finance. I could help others to start their own business and support them to reach their professional goals, rather than their fitness ones.

I moved to working part-time as a finance manager for a company and so found myself in a situation where I had both financial security and time. This seemed like the right moment to set up my own accounting business, so I began planning.

I studied under ACCA and AAT but when I set up my own practice I decided to move to The Institute of Certified Bookkeepers as I wanted to help small businesses and individuals and they seemed the best professional body to support me to do that. It allowed me to offer all the services I wanted – bookkeeping, payroll, VAT. self-assessment, annual accounts, corporation tax and advisory. So, I transferred over and set up my own bookkeeping and accounting business.

My business is called Lava Sky Accounting. Being outside under a big, open sky is my happy place and I love a beautiful sunset, so the name seemed a good fit. And like many triathletes, I'd love to one day visit to town of Kona on Hawaii's Big Island – the home of both stunning lava field vistas and the Ironman World Championship. Plus I couldn't think of another name that meant something to me!

The business started with mainly individuals or small companies but covering a range of sectors, which kept it interesting. However I soon moved the focus to sports coaches and fitness professionals as I felt my knowledge and experience of this area is a real asset. By developing a niche, I can combine my accounting expertise and love of fitness to offer clients a better service, especially any fellow endurance athletes.

For me, the biggest challenge is networking and lead generation. I'm great conversing with numbers but shy, and even a little phobic, when it comes to putting myself out there and making new contacts with potential clients. By narrowing my focus towards like-minded individuals (I can talk endurance sports all day) I'm able to create genuine connections, which leads to great professional relationships.

My proudest moment in business has been taking the step to set up my own bookkeeping business. It can be so easy to find reasons not to do things or put it off to another day or another year. Just like with exercising, the hardest part is getting yourself out the door. Once you do, you always feel better for it.

I have found the most important thing when deciding to take the plunge is to be honest with yourself. You will know deep down if this is what you truly want or if it is a case of the 'grass is greener'. If it is what you want, then don't be scared to go for it. Do lots of research and seek out support from others who have been there. Don't procrastinate, instead, set yourself targets and timelines – plan your roadmap for success but don't be disheartened if you face a few hurdles.

For me, starting a business is like entering a triathlon. You get those who always talk about doing it then find an excuse not to commit. Then there are those who enter but don't focus on their training and might not even make it to the start line. Finally, there are those who enter, commit fully to the training, complete the event and exceed their own expectations. Out of the three groups, it's the latter who gets the most enjoyment, satisfaction and biggest sense of achievement.

B
O
O
K
K
E
E
P
E
R
S'

S
T
O
R
I
E
S

It's this positive momentum that's crucial for a successful bookkeeping and accounting business. So go all in and see where it takes you.

Connect with Luna

www.lavasky.co.uk

Facebook: @lavaskyaccounting

LinkedIn: linkedin.com/company/68854563

Annabel Barnes - Bluebells Bookkeeping Ltd

BOOKKEEPERS' STORIES

Accounts have always been a big part of my life. I remember seeing my mum doing her books on the dining room table in big red books from when she ran her own businesses, so it was only natural that I wanted to follow in her footsteps.

I completed my AAT whilst working for a mental healthcare provider. I stayed with them for ten years, before moving to a micropigmentation training provider to manage their finance department.

My journey into becoming an independent bookkeeper started due to the lockdown in March 2020. My son has a congenital heart defect, which means he is potentially quite vulnerable. He had open-heart surgery at five months old, so when the COVID lockdowns were announced, we had no idea how this would affect my son's health. After many discussions with my husband (who was a keyworker at the time), we had the idea to set up my own bookkeeping practice. It would give us the flexibility to look after the children during lockdown. I approached my employer at the time and discussed our idea to see whether they would support me whilst I waited for my licence to come through. Thankfully, they agreed, and I remained employed to manage the finance department, whilst my licence arrived. The support and encouragement that my employer provided was amazing, and I couldn't have done it without them.

My business is called Bluebells Bookkeeping Ltd, and we are based in East Grinstead, West Sussex. We have clients varying in all shapes and sizes from small sole traders to large limited companies. We specialise in three different industries, beauty (including hairdressing), construction, facilities & trade and the care industry (often nurseries and childminders to those with learning disabilities).

There have been two stand out moments in business so far. The first was when I was asked to become a Director of a not-for-profit Community Interest Company that I voluntarily did the bookkeeping for (Non-Verbal Affective Care CIC). It was a great honour to be asked. The second moment was simply starting the business and the moment it became viable as it has allowed my husband to leave his job of 16 years and join the family business.

I would say the hardest part is getting started. I struggled with not believing in myself or that I was worthy enough to start a business. I had this thought many times but decided in the end to just go for it. I knew that I would always regret it if I didn't try. It's been the best decision I made. If I had to, I would do it all again.

I found it helpful to surround myself with a like-minded and supportive community. The 6 Figure Bookkeeper community has been amazing and so supportive. The 6 Month Success Programme definitely provides all the tools to help you grow a successful business and takes you through each step.

I am so pleased that I found the community at the start of my journey. I know that the business wouldn't have gotten to this point without the help and support of this community as well as Jo and Zoe.

Connect with Annabel

www.bluebellsbookkeeping.co.uk

Facebook: @bluebellsbookkeeping

Instagram: @bluebells_bookkeeping

Vicki Boddice - Boddice Accounting

Helping others is a huge part of my life. It's one of the things that led me into accounting. However, accounting also offers me the opportunity to be a role model to my daughter and support my husband to fulfil his dreams too. I'm very close with my family and want to provide them with as much help as they have given me over the years. I play wheelchair basketball and that really gets my competitive juices flowing. I'm also a qualified nail technician and love the creative side of doing nail art. Through these personal interests and my career, I want to prove to others that physical and mental disabilities don't need to limit you.

For the majority of my career, I specialised in insolvency and worked in many different big firms. However, after a breakdown 12 months ago, I gave up work. As my mental health is still recovering, and I am a wheelchair user, it was difficult to imagine I would succeed in a job where I had to conform to someone else's requirements. By setting up myself in business, I can control the type of clients I have and the advice being given. I also get autonomy over where I work and when.

I launched Boddice Accounting in July 2021 from my home in Falkirk - just between Glasgow and Edinburgh. I realised that my passion was helping other people to live their best lives. I realised so many women feel side-lined by other accountancy firms, especially those in the health and beauty industry. As a result, I decided that I would set up and focus on female-run start-up businesses, although I'd help anyone who needed me. I wanted to support people to get back to doing what they loved, rather than being stressed by their accounts.

The biggest challenge for me has been believing I am worth my rates. I also had to work on how to demonstrate that I am different to other firms by marketing myself effectively. This didn't come naturally to me, but I have now realised it's an essential part of the business. More recently, it was a pleasure to be asked to take part in an AccountingWeb webinar as a rising star in the field – definitely a career highlight!

Connect with Vicki

www.boddiceaccounting.co.uk
Facebook: @boddiceaccounting
Instagram: @boddice_accounting
LinkedIn: linkedin.com/in/vicki-boddice

B
O
O
K
K
E
E
P
E
R
S'

S
T
O
R
I
E
S

Jaime Bolton - All Cloud Accounting

When I was working for a building company in 2016, I was asked by one of the sub-contractors to prepare his accounts for his accountant. My career in bookkeeping started from there.

I always wanted to do accounts and was chuffed when he asked me to help him. Since the beginning of this year, things really took off thanks to the 6 Figure Bookkeeper and joining the Bookkeepers' 6 Month Success Programme. I now run my own practice which gives me the freedom to have control over my own working patterns. I can take and pick my daughter up from school every day, which is the main reason I started the business as I don't want to miss out on my daughter growing up. I want to be there at her sports days, Christmas nativity, and any other events that form part of her childhood. I never want to have to say that mummy can't come as she can't get the time off work. Now I know that will never happen, it drives me to make the practice a success so we can make memories as a family.

I run All Cloud Accounting based in Ilfracombe, North Devon. I have a variety of clients from a taxi firm to a second-hand mobile phone shop. My niche, however, is the construction industry. I have chosen this niche as I worked as an office manager for a building firm for five years. I single-handedly ran the office, covering everything relevant to accounts, payroll and CIS returns. My husband is also in the building trade, so I do all his paperwork as well. I like the construction trades, but I know some bookkeepers don't like dealing with CIS as it puts them off. In my experience it's not as bad as people think – I find it quite easy now. The only problem I have is that I find contractors and sub-contractors don't like keeping hold of their paperwork. This can make bookkeeping a bit of a challenge!

I have been running my practice since 2016 as a side hustle. In January 2021, I took it full time. Over this period the main challenge I have faced was being made redundant from a part-time role in an accountancy firm. I was on minimum wage, but I didn't mind as I was learning how to compile year end accounts for self-assessments amongst learning other skills. At the time, I didn't have enough clients to make working for myself a full-time job. I was also getting married the following year, so I had to get another full-time job which was in sales ledger. I hated it as I knew I was more capable than churning out sales invoices all day. Whilst I was doing this job, I was trying to grow my business on the side so I could eventually leave my paid employment and do what I love and be a full-time bookkeeper whilst working from home.

I think the proudest moment is when I received my practice license. I am still studying so I hope to have limited companies added to my license in the not too distant future.

What would I say to somebody who wants to start a practice? If you are starting a practice you need to be visible across social media. It's important to be yourself on these platforms as people buy from people, especially those who they know like and trust. Someone could follow you for a whole year before they are ready to use your services. There are no shortcuts to success and sometimes it takes a while to find clients. It has taken me five years to get to where I am now, but I couldn't be prouder of what I've achieved.

Connect with Jaime

www.allcloudaccounting.co.uk

Facebook & Instagram @allcloudaccounting

Linkedin: linkedin.com/in/jaime-bolton-aatqb-33858341

Alison Bryan - Flourish Accounts

I would say that I am a perfectionist and also like to help people. This has shaped the way I do business as my ultimate goal is to be an outstanding bookkeeper and to help businesses to flourish. When I am not working, I am conscious of my health and fitness. I am a keen exerciser and enjoy eating well. I have a son (16) and a husband (62) and we love to travel. Being self-employed gives me the freedom to do just that. If there is a big holiday coming up, then I can earn extra when I need to. But also, I can take time off to spend the earnings on travel when I want to!

I have always been in some form of accounting. I worked in the City of London for 16 years in various management accounting roles. When my son started school, I opted for a change in pace and worked in the finance department for a school. I studied for the AAT back in 1991 and then refreshed my skills in 2010 by studying for the IAB. Since 2010, I have been self-employed and never looked back.

The main reason that I started my practice was to be in control of my work. I think this is quite a natural trait of accountants – we like to know what's going on! However, it also allowed me more say in the way I did things in both my personal and professional life. I am now the sole owner of Flourish Accounts, which has been running for 12 years now. I have 57 clients across a range of sectors from building firms to beauticians to eCommerce. I enjoy the range of clients, and I don't have a niche at present. I am based in Hornchurch - the last London borough before it becomes Essex.

My proudest moment as a bookkeeper has been becoming self-employed. It was a challenge, but I remain fully motivated to work long hours without being distracted. This often means saying no to those that think self-employment means I can meet every day for coffee or lunch.

For anyone looking to start their own bookkeeping business, my one piece of advice is to just do it. It's also important to keep faith in the business and your abilities. One client quickly turns into two which soon turns into 10…

Connect with Alison

www.flourishaccounts.com

Instagram @flourishaccounts

LinkedIn: linkedin.com/in/alison-bryan-fmaat-fiab-41820b5

Caroline Cant - CC Virtual Bookkeeping

B
O
O
K
K
E
E
P
E
R
S'

S
T
O
R
I
E
S

I am a mum of two girls and ultimately they are my why. I have a desire to provide for them financially and I trained as a bookkeeper to create a life of balance between working and being there for them.

I am a fully qualified nail technician and ran my own mobile salon very briefly. While I was studying for my bookkeeping qualifications, I worked in various administrative and finance roles part time.

My favourite subjects at school were Art and Maths and I was always torn between the two. I left school half way through sixth form and decided to go to to College and study to be a Nail Technician, once qualified I started my own mobile business but soon I fell pregnant and decided it wasn't going to work. I studied with the ICB after my first was born and worked part time for a charity as their Finance Officer until I passed my level 3. After my second daughter was born I accidentally fell into self employment as a bookkeeper and my business has grown from there.

My business is called CC Virtual Bookkeeping and I work with service based clients. I niche within the creative sector, I particularly enjoy working with women, designers and online businesses.

Running a business is a challenge in itself because although I knew how to do the bookkeeping, I didn't necessarily know how to build and run a business at all. There is an awful lot to think about and there is only one of me.

My top three challenges have to be:

1. Visibility: I've found making myself visible to potential clients very difficult because I'm quite introverted by nature.

2. Pricing: quoting my worth and knowing the value I'm adding, and

3. Systems: deciding what tools I need in my business without spending a fortune on software and subscriptions.

There is definitely an element of shiny new object syndrome to contend with, but starting your own bookkeeping business is definitely worth it, and with the right support network you don't have to do it alone.

When I was volunteering as treasurer for my daughters pre school, through my knowledge I was able to help pull them back from the brink of closure and that has to be my proudest moment.

It was really hard work with no monetary benefit but it was so worth it. I learnt so much from that experience.

Connect with Caroline

www.ccvirtualbookkeeping.com

Facebook & Instagram: @ccvirtualbookkeeping

BOOKKEEPERS' STORIES

Alexis Charkiw – Right Click Accounting

I've always enjoyed helping other business owners with their accounts, queries and taking someone from being afraid of doing their accounts to feeling confident. I truly believe every business owner should know what's happening with their numbers but I understand that approaching an Accountant you don't know can be overwhelming. This passion came to light when in May 2019 I was in Croatia to get married. The night before my wedding I was reconciling my own business accounts in Xero and my now husband said, 'you love doing accounts don't you. I think you should do it for other people because that's what you really enjoy'. I registered my practice the next month.

Before I started my practice, I worked for Barclays in Corporate Banking, predominantly in the Risk Control and Credit Unit. I did my AAT qualification in the evenings while working full time. Then in 2014 I had twins and paying for two lots of childcare wasn't viable but for me, neither was being a stay at home Mum - I love my children but going from a busy corporate career to staying at home all day was a huge personal challenge. So I started a product subscription business from the kitchen table. It was a great business, a steep learning curve and we sold over 6000 boxes worldwide. In January 2020 I suspended subscriptions because an opportunity presented itself. I co-founded a business that secured a six figure budget from the Welsh Government to run a pilot project of a time and skill swapping app. I held Board meetings, took minutes, managed the project and budget. The app successfully launched in June 2021. I then left the business to pursue my practice full time.

My ideal clients are directors of Limited Companies that have been trading for 12 months or more. They're at the stage of scaling or recruiting so I focus on what actions are required to put that in place and focus on automation as much as possible. They're also aware of the needs to do accounts but aren't currently using the numbers to make business decisions. Most of my clients are amazing at their craft but need support and guidance with the business and finance sides of the company.

I've had many proud moments, but I think the one that stands out is when I created my own website and got the subscription and payment plugin to work properly. It took me hours (I just didn't have the budget to outsource it) and I finished it at 3am. I was so excited that I jumped around the room but nobody saw that triumph because everyone was asleep! Sometimes it's the small things you remember because that's where you have the biggest growth as a business owner.

If you're thinking of starting a bookkeeping business, my advice would be not to be afraid to pivot if you want to change direction. I don't mean changing your mind every time it gets hard or getting distracted by the next trending idea but just like an employee wants a promotion or new challenge, sometimes you get to the end of that chapter in your business and want to do something new and that's completely ok.

Connect with Alexis

www.rightclickaccounting.com

Instagram: @alexisrightclick

Facebook Group: @groups/rightclickwithalexis

Linkedin: linkedin.com/in/charkiwalexis/

Carly Clark - Conquer Accountancy

B
O
O
K
K
E
E
P
E
R
S'

S
T
O
R
I
E
S

I have one son and aside from working I have started running and really enjoy seeing my Personal Trainer every week. I also love walking our dog every day and exploring new walks!

I am an Accountant and worked in a Finance department in industry (stockbroking) for 21 years before I started my own practice. I have always wanted to work for myself and when I was made redundant decided that was the best time to take the leap.

My business is Conquer Accountancy. I have various clients but try to niche in industries which help and support others. This means I tend to work with physios, personal trainers, and childrens' class providers. I've been running the business for 18 months and the biggest challenges I've faced to get to this point are getting trained up on bookkeeping software and researching all of the tools that are out there to help you run a practice. Having worked in a very old fashioned business before, I had only ever used desktop Sage and Excel!

**B
O
O
K
K
E
E
P
E
R
S'

S
T
O
R
I
E
S**

I feel incredibly proud when I'm referred by current clients to their peers - I hope it means they are happy with my service and to anyone thinking of starting their own bookkeeping business, I'd suggest speaking to others who have been on the same journey, and having your software decisions made before you start. It's hard to find the time to do research once work starts rolling in.

Connect with Carly

Facebook: @Conquer-Accountancy-103623764927588

Leah Crowfoot - LC Virtual FD Ltd

I have been working in finance since the age of 19. I started work in Ernst & Young as the post lady, which led me into working in a bank. I then moved into industry between the ages of 21 to 36 and started my training.

I have always wanted to work for myself, but I never dared to do it. Then the pandemic hit and the imposed isolation that was put on my son who started nursery in September 2020, meant that being both an employee and being there for my children just didn't work, my employer did not like me taking time off work, and being at home alone with a one-year-old and a three-year-old meant it was impossible to get anything done.

Combined with the encouragement of the people around me within The 6 Figure Bookkeepers Club and my family and friends, I finally took the plunge in March 2021.It is the best thing I have ever done!

I'm motivated by my family, and my job works around them. Not the other way around. I work my own hours so that I can be there for the school drop off and pick up. I can also take time off as and when it is the school holidays.

My business is called LC Virtual FD Ltd and we are based in Dudley, West Midlands. My practice officially opened in March 2021. I work with a variety of business owners but they are all looking for a way to understand their business finances better. As an eco-warrior and a spiritualist, I love to work with like-minded business owners.

One of my biggest challenges has been having the confidence to put myself out there. I am naturally a very shy and reserved person, but to get noticed you need to shout. There is a lot of noise and competition on social media, where I do most of my marketing and sales work.

I've also had to get a clear picture of what I actually want to do with my business. There is so much that can be done as an Accountant and Bookkeeper. It has taken me a long time to actually define what brings me joy in my work, my practice and its offerings have grown beyond anything I could have ever imagined all with the support of the amazing people who I surround myself with.

All the hard work has finally paid off as one of my proudest moments has been getting my first client that wasn't a friend or family member. I knew that they were employing me for my skills and what I could offer, rather than because they knew me. Getting known for who I was, as well as what I can do has helped me to believe in myself and my business even more than I could ever know.

One of the main things that have helped me is to surround myself with like-minded people. I'd advise others to not be afraid of mixing with other Bookkeepers or even Accountants. As a collective, they have been there, done that and got the t-shirt for most of the issues you are going to face. Making wise investments in my personal growth, as well as the business growth, has also been crucial. Having the right support behind you is worth every penny!

Connect with Leah

www.lcvirtualfdltd.com

Facebook Personal @crowfoot.leah

Facebook Group @lcbusinessfinanceschool

Facebook & Instagram @lcvirtualfdltd

LinkedIn: linkedIn.com/in/leahcrowfoot

Leanda Daddow - Celtic Bookkeeping & Accountancy Services Ltd

Before I became a bookkeeper, I had a variety of roles from hunting for mines in the Royal Navy to being a bank clerk. I was also an accounts assistant at a law firm.

I've been in practice for 11 years now. I started the business when I was already doing my husband's books. I lost my job for being over-qualified and vowed never to work for anyone again.

Celtic Bookkeeping & Accountancy Services Ltd works mainly with tradespeople and those with property portfolios. Many of our clients fall into both categories. With a love of the outdoors and wellbeing, we work closely with people in the outdoor and fitness world too. Although I am based in a small seaside village in Cornwall, because we are digital and work remotely, we can cover the whole of the UK. This is great for improving our reach and means that we have a huge potential customer base.

Over the past few years, I have suffered a sequence of family bereavements. Not unsurprisingly, this had a massive impact on my mental health. I pushed myself to keep the wheels of my business going but lost control and almost shut the doors. I sunk to a level where I felt I had totally lost control. I was not charging adequately for my services and time. I recognised that I was continually firefighting and dealing with the clients that were shouting the loudest. Relying on a team where I had not implemented controls and processes, meant that I was not in control. When I was unable to cope with day-to-day activities, I was not aware of any issues that were arising with staff. As I had no time, I wasn't looking after and valuing them on an individual level either. By charging extremely low fees, I was not covering the time and costs, which compounded the issues and added further pressure.

My biggest success has been building my minimum monthly fee from £30 a month to £300 a month in 12 months. I've also reduced my client industries to specialise in certain areas. This has allowed me to live the life I want. It's provided me the ability to offer work to newly qualified bookkeepers and build their experience and skills. I envisage them eventually following in my footsteps to open and build their own practice. Having them support the business means that I am also able to do the school run and go for a run/ swim during the day should I feel the need. I feel it is important to set a goal that you want to achieve outside of work – even if it's something simple like being able to do the school run consistently. This will help you align your business goals to provide you with the life you want to live.

By training our staff well and giving them a level of autonomy, I know that my clients are looked after and my whole team is singing from the same hymn sheet. By installing processes to follow, we ensure that we are all working towards the same goals for our clients.

Part of the reason for our success has been in the approach to scaling the business. When starting, my advice would be to document all processes and begin to produce a manual of how you work. This will make expanding and outsourcing much easier.

Connect with Leanda

www.celticbookkeeping.co.uk
Facebook: @celticbookkeeping,
LinkedIn: linkedin.com/in/leanda-daddow-82a8a195/

Laura Day-Henderson - More Than Bookkeeping

B
O
O
K
K
E
E
P
E
R
S'

S
T
O
R
I
E
S

Like most of us, I didn't spend my younger years dreaming of working in finance, quite the opposite... I remember being upset when I was little as I desperately wanted to be a binman but realised I was a girl (..so glad we now live in the 21st century..!).

Whilst I was busy chasing my wildest ambitions, everyone else was noticing my mathematic ability. If I received 1p for every person who declared I'd be an accountant, I'd be a millionaire! I knew I wasn't good enough to achieve these expectations so I avoided accountancy at all costs because not attempting to become an accountant meant I couldn't disappoint by failing to achieve their aspirations for me.

The problem was, they were correct! I was destined to work my magic with numbers in life! I resisted their wisdom, but eventually, after relocating to Wales, I'd run out of jobs that didn't require me to drive or speak Welsh - the only other jobs available were finance-based. So I successfully applied for an 'accounts assistant' role despite being honest that I had absolutely no experience (but declared I can make a decent cuppa!).

Unfortunately, a few months later, a bad car accident left me unable to work for quite some time. We moved back to Yorkshire whilst I recovered and once I was ready to return back to work, I knew exactly what I wanted to do – accountancy!

Since then, I've worked in quite broad roles in industry, empowering businesses of all sizes (from start-ups to larger organisations such as the NHS) to grow, transform their financial health and automate their processes so that they can continue to do what they do best whilst being assured the financial side of things was in the safety of my clumsy but meticulous hands.

I loved transforming these businesses but knew I could create a much wider impact.

I also desperately wanted better flexibility around my family, health and energy levels. I craved a better work-life balance (less 20+ hour days, more adventures!). However, having the financial stability of a safe and attractive salary stopped me from following my dreams.

Thankfully fate took control of things and after working 20+ hour days throughout Covid, my loyalty and hard-work was rewarded.. ..with redundancy! It was the best Christmas present as it gave me the opportunity to take the risk I'd been desperate to take – to become self-employed and start working on my terms!

The only problem was... I loved all things finance, but knew from the get-go that building a traditional bookkeeping/accountancy practice wouldn't work for me. Thankfully, we don't need to follow the status quo, we simply need to do something we are passionate about and that relieves a pain point for our customers.

I created More Than Bookkeeping in 2021, combining my passion (mentoring others) with my expertise (advisory services). I love that something so enjoyable counts as work!

I teach and support bookkeepers and accountants to empower their clients to develop, grow and adapt through "advisory" services which in turn generates both the bookkeeper/accountant and client more revenue and profit. I also offer a comfort blanket to bookkeepers/accountants by mentoring them to support with any technical queries and offer a 'done for you' advisory service for those who want to empower their clients but don't have the capacity to do it themselves.

I now work the hours that work for me (resting when I need to and working when my energy levels allow). We take a day-off mid-week and explore somewhere new and exciting. Sometimes (perhaps a little too often!) we also take a few hours off mid-day to go somewhere nice. We have the flexibility to work from anywhere signal allows so our office will soon have a backdrop of dramatic mountain ranges, tranquil lakes, glorious sunrises and the most distracting views!

Work now revolves around my life, rather than my life having to revolve around my work.

My lack of confidence and self-belief held me back from creating the dream life I yearned after for far too long.

Confidence and self-belief are funny things – no matter how much 'evidence' you have to dispute it, a pesky voice tells you you're not good enough, don't know enough, aren't experienced enough. Past successes were just flukes. Kind words people have said about you are because they feel sorry for you. I could be here all day, however, I know your voice tells you these same things too as unfortunately we are human!

This has had a significant knock-on effect as I've held back thousands of business owners too by not supporting those bookkeepers/accountants who desperately needed my expertise to help them better support their clients and in turn the economy – how selfish of me!

It's so important to surround yourself with those who believe in you and remind you of what you are capable of, helping you quash that voice holding you back.

If you are thinking of becoming self-employed, use this opportunity to create the business that enables you to live the life of your wildest dreams. Whilst bookkeeping/accountancy practices are a fantastic way to achieve this, remember you don't have to follow the norm. If you have more specific passions then build a business that focuses on these - this may be niching to industries aligned with your passions or just offering services that you are a knowledgeable expert in.

Rather than worrying about what if it doesn't work, just imagine how amazing your life could be if it does work!

Connect with Laura

Website: morethanbookkeeping.support/
Facebook & Instagram: @MoreThanBookkeeping
Linkedin: www.linkedin.com/in/lauraday-henderson

BOOKKEEPERS' STORIES

B
O
O
K
K
E
E
P
E
R
S'

S
T
O
R
I
E
S

Nicola Fallon - Virtual Accounts and Taxes Ltd

Before I became a bookkeeper, I had lots of different roles. However, my main job was as a Payroll Manager. I was made redundant in September 2020, so during my notice period, I came up with the idea of setting up my own business. I was looking at opening my own payroll bureau at first, but after researching online what other people in the area were offering, I found out about Ideal Schools and the Institute of Certified Bookkeepers (ICB). This led me to decide on getting the qualifications I needed for a bookkeeping practice licence with the ICB.

The main motivation for setting up my practice was my family. I have a blended family with two sons from my first marriage, aged 23 and 21. I also have a stepdaughter, aged 16, with my husband, Mark. I grew up with three brothers and I have 12 aunties/uncles and 34 cousins. It's a big family, and they are a massive part of my life.

My practice is called Virtual Accounts and Taxes Ltd, based in Salford, near Manchester. I launched on 2nd August 2021.

My clients are local people with small businesses. It's mainly sole traders, but there are also some limited companies too. My niche is music and entertainment - I have a couple of singers as clients. Music is in my blood and it's something I'd like to have in common with my clients - even if they are just music fans like me.

My biggest challenge has been knowing where to start with setting up a business. It's all well and good getting the qualifications to become a bookkeeper and tax agent, but I knew nothing about setting up as an agent, insurance, branding, marketing, sales or even what software to use.

My proudest moment was being put forward by Ideal Schools for the ICB Student of the Year Luca Award and being one of five finalists in that category.

The secret behind some of my success is the preparation - preparation is key. My husband always says, "fail to prepare, then prepare to fail!". Our kids think it's really annoying, but it's so true! I would also suggest that others starting out shouldn't compare your journey or goals to someone else's - "you do you". Everybody is different and has different needs, so one person's small win is another person's big win; comparison is the thief of joy.

Connect with Nicola

virtualaccountsandtaxes.co.uk

Facebook: @virtualaccountsandtaxesltd

Instagram: @virtual_accounts_and_taxes

LinkedIn: linkedin.com/in/nicola-fallon-payroll-tax-accounting

Mark Farrington - Spiral Bookkeeping

Before I became a bookkeeper, I was doing plastering and home improvements around our hometown of Chatteris in Cambridgeshire. Becoming a bookkeeper might not seem like a natural progression from this career, but it's been a dream of mine to run a bookkeeping practice since I was in my mid-20s

I first started in finance when I became a temporary treasurer to my woodturning guild. I quickly got hooked. The former treasurer suggested I pursue bookkeeping, but I didn't think I was clever enough. She suggested that I do a course and learn, but I still believed you had to have attended university to train. Plus, I couldn't afford it at the time.

As many years passed by, my passion for bookkeeping never faded. Still, it took me a further 10 years for me to gain the courage to go back to studying. I didn't realise that studying whilst working is exceptionally hard work. It took me around nine years of studying to reach my dream. You could say that altogether I have worked for more than 20 years to achieve a bookkeeping business.

Something my family and I struggled with was finding a name for the business. I have some silly sayings and one of them is to 'work smart, not hard'. Living up to this, I recruited a professional to do the branding. It was a good move.

It's a bit unusual, but I love my hobby of woodturning. The shavings look like spirals when cut correctly on the lathe. So, after some discussion with the branding professional, we decided on the name of 'Spiral Bookkeeping'. It reflects the passion that my wife and I have for crafts, while still sounding professional.

At this point in time, I have one booking for a new client. As I'm a very new business there are no customers currently, but I'm confident this will soon change. At the moment I am targeting small businesses to build up my confidence. Once I have that confidence, then I will get stuck in. I am a bit of a workaholic so once we get these initial few clients, I'm sure we will go from strength to strength.

My challenges at this point in my journey have been getting up and running as well as deciding on my business name. I was very proud when after 20 years of believing I could do it, I finally got to upgrade my membership to MICB PM.dip. It was a small but incredibly satisfying moment when I got to add this to my email signature.

I know that it's extremely hard work to fit in becoming a bookkeeper with everyday life. However, I found it's important to not lose sight of that dream. I am living proof that you can do it and there is a fantastic bookkeeping community out there to offer you support along the way.

Connect with Mark

www.spiralbookkeeping.co.uk

Kathryn Frimond - Your Local Bookkeeper

Being a bookkeeper allows me to do the best for my family as well as work with sustainable/eco-conscious clients. It gives me a lot of flexibility to work around my own family commitments and health. I also hate to say it but trying to be the best motivates me to achieve new and great things!

Prior to bookkeeping, I worked for 10 years in corporate banking for two, top tier banks. I worked primarily in real-estate restructuring and recoveries for large corporate entities. This was a high-stress city job, which took its toll mentally. During my time here I saw lots of distressed businesses with one thing in common - poor cash flow. While not great for the businesses, it did strike me as a missed opportunity for better financial management.

Following maternity leave and redundancy, I retrained as a bookkeeper after some guidance from a careers coach. I chose to focus on using my corporate background in the recoveries sector to help clients avoid the situations I had seen, which led to company failures. My goal was to remediate problems with things like poor cash flow, a lack of awareness of company finances, and no management accounts or regular reviews.

My business is a virtual bookkeeping practice, "Your Local Bookkeeper". I run it from my home and office on the Surrey/Hampshire border.

I started wanting to be a virtual bookkeeper, focusing on being "local wherever you are". This has now evolved into a business helping clients which share my passion - leaving the planet in a better position than when we entered it. Whilst I still have other clients, I now focus my marketing on ethical, sustainable and purpose-led businesses. I typically work with local businesses, charities and a range of purpose-led companies.

I found that focusing on a specific type of client or niche meant that I was able to provide a better service. I am also able to work with clients that have the same values as me, creating some great networks and friendships as a result.

My biggest initial challenge was the pricing. I simply didn't know what to charge or how much was too much. Should you charge hourly? Monthly? As a package? After discovering the 6 Figure Bookkeeper and GoProposal, I'm now more confident in my pricing.

Since writing this book, my four-year-old son has been diagnosed with leukaemia. My biggest challenge now is managing a business alongside being a full-time carer for my son. I also have to look after myself and re-gain my work-life balance. I have found that having good systems in place with all the processes mapped out has helped subcontractors to pick up daily tasks. Processes, alongside software and a trusted group of other bookkeeping colleagues, has meant I can take a step back from the business without it impacting the day-to-day service. Due to the corporate structures I previously worked in, I would have only been able to take a limited time out of work. It wouldn't have been possible to change the business to suit my lifestyle. Obviously, my current situation gives me more flexibility.

While it might be hard in the beginning, working with clients that share your values will make the job a lot easier. As you are starting out the work is likely to be quieter, so this is a great time to set up your foundations and processes. It'll help to make sure you are ready when you are busier in the future. You shouldn't be afraid to outsource things you don't like doing.

If you join and fully participate in a group of like-minded bookkeepers and accountants - like 6 Figure Bookkeeper - other people's knowledge will help so much. You'll also make some great friends in the process.

Connect with Kathryn

www.localbookkeeper.co.uk

Facebook & Instagram: @your_local_bookkeeper

LinkedIn: linkedin.com/in/kathryn-frimond

B
O
O
K
K
E
E
P
E
R
S'

S
T
O
R
I
E
S

Kristy Glenister - 4cast Bookkeeping Limited

The thing that motivated me to start my own bookkeeping practice was providing for my family. However, that motivation has changed. Now, I just love what I'm doing. Helping other people to make sense of their numbers in a friendly way brings me a lot of professional and personal satisfaction.

Before I became a Bookkeeper, I had a number of different positions. I started off working in a junior administrator role and then became a legal secretary. Whilst working as a legal secretary, I discovered my love of technology and I moved into the IT department. I got to be involved with each different department within the firm and I enjoyed the challenges that it brought every day. However, when we decided to start a family, I started working from home to run the admin side of my partner's business. It was at this time that I discovered bookkeeping.

I had never thought of running my own business before but one day, our Accountant called me to see if I would be interested in some work to sort out someone's books. I was stunned, to say the least, but the seed had been planted.

I'm not the kind of person to do things by halves, so I immediately started looking into bookkeeping qualifications and came across the ICB. I then signed up for their Level 2 qualification and my journey began. I was so nervous when I began my course, I wasn't looking forward to taking exams after more years than I would care to mention! However, I soon got the bug and began making solid progress. I took my final Level 3 exams during lockdown and took one exam twice even though I had passed it the first time but due to the distraction of having everyone at home, I didn't achieve the score that I knew I was capable of. So after much deliberation with my Tutor and the ICB telling me that my original score was great, I still decided I would regret it if I hadn't achieved my best result. I took the exam again and was so pleased I did!

After passing my ICB Level 3 qualification I setup my Practice. I am now the proud owner/director of 4cast Bookkeeping Limited. I currently have a small number of fabulous clients and I am based in Buckinghamshire in the middle of the Chiltern Hills. My practice is virtual, which enables me to service more clients in a far more efficient way whilst still being able to spend time with my family and taking time out to walk my dog.

My main business challenge is finding new clients. I find it very difficult to know what to post on social media and how to get myself out there. However, I am slowly getting better at this but in the

B
O
O
K
K
E
E
P
E
R
S'

S
T
O
R
I
E
S

meantime, I'm loving learning about marketing and all the other aspects of running my own business. It is challenging at times but knowing that all the processes and systems that I'm implementing are the foundations of a great business keeps me motivated (and a little bit obsessed).

Now I'm heading to the end of my second year in Practice and it is so rewarding to see my clients' businesses grow year on year. Bookkeeping has brought me a lot of purpose and a solid vocation not to mention many new friends. I'd definitely encourage anyone who was thinking about it to take it up.

Connect with Kristy

www.4castbookkeeping.co.uk

Facebook: @4castbookkeeping

Twitter: @4castB

Instagram: @4castbookkeeping

LinkedIn: linkedin.com/in/kristy-glenister-micb-78566733

LinkedIn: linkedin.com/company/4castbookkeeping

Nikki Hackett - N.E Bookkeeping

BOOKKEEPERS' STORIES

My motivation in becoming a bookkeeper is my family. I want to be around more for the kids, doing the school runs and seeing them grow up. My partner works away in the week, so he misses a lot of family time. I want to be successful so that he can work closer to home. I love seeing friends and having a bit of adult time when we can all find a date we can make. I love to read and I'm a big Harry Potter fan, although I can't possibly love it more than my daughter does.

Before I was a bookkeeper, I worked in banking for 15 years at RBS dealing with credit cards and bank accounts. It was a lot of customer service and admin work. I had various different roles during my time there. I was a team manager and then went on to work in projects. I also travelled to India for a month to help train new staff.

I've always been interested in bookkeeping but didn't make the leap until I was made redundant in 2017. I had gained bookkeeping qualifications with IAB and then decided to study AAT. My end goal is to become an accountant, so I can do accounts from start to finish rather than outsource some of the work.

My business is called N.E Bookkeeping, and we're based in Shoebury, Essex. The business got the name as there was originally two of us (Nikki and Emma). Emma decided it wasn't the right thing for her and pulled out, but I continued the business on my own and decided to keep the name. My other half came up with the name and slogan of "Any Bookkeeping, Anywhere" which is a play on the business name. My clients are in various industries, including construction, lingerie, plumbing/electrics and yacht chartering. My niche is with family-run businesses as all my clients have it in common. I can relate to them and their needs because I know what it's like to run a business around my family whilst working a part-time job too.

I have been running the business since August/September 2019. I got my first client in January 2020. I made the decision at the start of 2021 that I was going to put everything into my business and make it successful so that I could resign from my employed job. I got another two clients in April 2021 from being more visible on social media. A previous employer now subcontracts their bookkeeping work to me and in 2022 my goal is to give up the employed job.

My proudest achievement on top of gaining my AAT level 4 qualification has been getting two new clients within two days of each other. My biggest challenge is still getting clients. I am slowly getting more confident in selling my service, which has been greatly helped by improving my visibility on social media. I have also joined a local networking group to try and get myself known. Putting myself out there is massively out of my comfort zone, but I need to do it to help my business to succeed.

I'd say if starting a bookkeeping practice is something that you want, then you need to keep going until you achieve it. Finding a community of like-minded people to get help and advice from is really important. You shouldn't be scared to ask questions, it's likely someone else is thinking the same thing and simply doesn't want to ask.

Connect with Nikki

www.ne-bookkeeping.co.uk

Facebook: @nebookkeeping1

Instagram: @n.e.bookkeeping

LinkedIn: linkedin.com/nikkihackettbookkeepermiab

Donna Haslewood - Artisan Accountant & Co

I am a wife and mum to two beautiful girls. We live next to the sea, which has always been one of my lifelong dreams. We all love the water and go swimming or bodyboarding whenever we get the chance.

I consider myself a very creative person, so I love doing anything artistic with my family. This might include painting pottery to making our own pictures or Christmas cards. I always find one of the best ways I relax is to simply sit and draw in my bullet journal or sketchbook. It's my natural comfort zone and one of my life's pleasures. We also love to go camping and explore new places. The kids love seeing more of the world and having fresh adventures.

Prior to becoming a bookkeeper, I worked as a Finance Officer in the NHS. However, when I was in college and university, I studied

Media and Interactive Design. On paper, it wasn't the most natural progression!

Whilst working in the NHS, I was lucky to be offered an opportunity to study AAT. The Trust gave me day release to complete levels 2 and 3. I then fell pregnant. Soon after, I found I couldn't go back to my role in the NHS following maternity leave as part-time/flexible working wasn't an option. The cost of nursery broke even with my paid work, so it didn't feel right leaving my daughter in nursery to go to work. Especially when we wouldn't be financially better off for doing so. I had no alternative but to leave employment. During my maternity year, I decided to complete my AAT qualification with level 4 as this gave me options for the future. My husband was then offered a new job, which meant we had to relocate from South Wales to Norfolk. Once we had settled into our new life in Norfolk with a new home and a young baby, I began seeking out job opportunities but struggled with the location of the roles (30 mins away) or because they only offered full-time hours. This didn't suit our family logistics. At this point, I decided to look into setting up my own business.

Now, I run Artisan Accountant & Co. We've been in business for eight years and specialise in the artisan/handmade creative market. This means I get to engage with my hobbies as my job and work with like-minded people. I am based in Gorleston-on-Sea, Norfolk.

Like many self-employed people, one of the biggest challenges has been juggling my business around family life. The recent pandemic has meant that I had to home school my two children.

It was great to spend more time with them, but I also gained a great deal of respect for teachers. In 2020, I also had to manage my business around my own personal diagnosis of bone cancer and a major operation to treat this.

My proudest moments in business are when I see the clients that I work with grow stronger. I get a big kick out of seeing them want to take control and understand the numbers more. One great example was when I saved a client £8k on her tax bill after noticing she was incorrectly reconciling her sales, causing double sales. She was pretty motivated to get on top of her finances after that!

I think the most important thing is to get your license in place first, and then just go for it! Businesses in today's climate are more in need of bookkeepers than they realise. It's your job to show them that!

Connect with Donna

www.artisanaccountantandco.co.uk

Facebook: @artisanaccountantandco

Instagram: @artisan_accountant_co

Julie Holland - Blu Bookkeeping

I'm a mother of three with two granddaughters. I love walking and exploring the countryside. I'm also a bit of a history buff and enjoy visiting castles and their grounds. I belong to English Heritage, so we get into most castles for free. I love houseplants, but this year my kids say I've made my living room like a jungle!

In creating the business, I wanted something that supports me but also gives me the freedom to do what I want as I am fiercely independent. I'm always keen to develop the business and find one of the best ways is by learning new things from YouTube.

I've always worked in finance since I left school. My first job after leaving school was with Lloyds Bank. I achieved my AAT level 2 but never completed level 3 because of family issues and so I left learning. Instead, I learnt everything from the ground up and became qualified by experience. My last job before starting the business was as a Financial Controller – though I've never looked back!

BOOKKEEPERS' STORIES

I've always wanted to work for myself but never had the confidence. This was especially more so when I hit menopause and my confidence hit rock bottom. I felt I let my career falter.

When COVID struck I got sent home for Lockdown one. During Lockdown two, I was furloughed. Having all that time on my hands, while still on full pay, meant that I could do a course with Training Link and get qualified as a bookkeeper. Now I have got my license and have left my job, moved back to Reading, I'm now ready to advance the business.

My business is Blu Bookkeeping and we're based in Purley-on-Thames near Reading. I'd previously worked for two franchise pest control companies, so most of my clients are Pest Controllers. It's a pretty unusual niche, but it's one I know well.

My biggest challenges are faced by so many new businesses: Lack of experience in marketing, lack of clients and not much budget to spend. I've worked hard to build my business over the past eight months and my proudest moment so far has been finding the confidence to create monthly P&L videos for my clients, mostly because I hate my picture being taken and being in the limelight.

Connect with Julie

Facebook: @BluBookkeeping

LinkedIn: linkedin.com/julie-holland-blubookkeeping

YouTube: @channel/UCm4KpfoI5IaWcKXJ66z_19w

Tracy Jeffreys - Grove Virtual Services

B
O
O
K
K
E
E
P
E
R
S'

S
T
O
R
I
E
S

I love spending time with my husband, son and two labradors. Getting quality time with them has always been difficult in the past but moving forward we have got lots planned. My favourite place to visit is Cromer in Norfolk. I have just found a love of Tai Chi. I really love interior design and houses and making things. My mum taught me how to sew, so I make my own blinds, cushions and lampshades among other handicrafts.

Before I became a bookkeeper, I had many different eclectic roles. I was a merchandiser/buyer, civil servant (data analyst) and a data manager for electric bus stop signs. When I met my husband and had my son, I had to work part-time in cafes, shops and bars as we moved around a lot. My confidence went. My last job was as a part-time bookkeeper in a carpet shop. After that, I began upholstering chairs and making interior accessories to sell at craft fairs.

Whilst moving around the country, I thought about becoming a bookkeeper to fit around my family. I used to do the bookkeeping for our rental property, so it felt like a sensible next step. Subsequently, I started my AAT level 2 and got the job in the carpet shop. After some time, I left that position to help my dad to support my mum who was living with dementia. I thought it would be easy looking after her while studying for my ICB. However, I underestimated how bad my anxiety was.

When I started as a bookkeeper, I just called myself 'Jeffreys Bookkeeping Services' (original, right?). While I had set the business up, I didn't really do anything with it. It largely just sat there. In explanation, my mum had just died and I thought I could start a business, carry on studying, cope with my husband's PTSD and help my dad all at the same time. I now realise that I was overstretching myself as that was a lot to try and do simultaneously. Initially, it didn't work out and my anxiety got worse. I sought help for grief and anxiety before my dad died. He later died in March, and shortly after I found out about the Bookkeepers' 6 Month Success Programme. Since joining it, I have rebranded and renamed. I also decided on a niche of interior designers.

I'm now Grove Virtual Services and based in Oldcotes, Worksop.

One of the biggest challenges has been knowing where to start with the practicalities of starting a business and marketing it effectively. I wasn't sure who to ask for advice. Trying to study at the same time meant that I had limited time to find out and that I had other factors vying for my attention. I'm so proud that after the rebrand and hard work that the business has re-established itself and I am personally in a much better place.

I have found that the most important thing to support your success is finding a bookkeeping community that you feel comfortable in. At points, you will feel that you don't know what you are doing and that you can't do it. You might even think about stopping and working for someone else instead. It's important to have this community around you to support you at these times and to act as a living demonstration people can succeed with it. They will also help you to remember why you are doing this. It is hard but it's also enjoyable.

Connect with Tracy

www.grovevirtualservices.co.uk

Facebook: @GroveVirtualServices

Instagram: @grovevirtualservices

LinkedIn: inkedin.com/in/tracy-jeffreys-8a58961b5

Pintrest: @grovevirtualservices/_created/

Claire Johnson - Bluebell Bookkeeping and Admin

Having grown up on a farm and having a mum who worked in a bank before marrying my dad, I guess it was inevitable that I'd be encouraged into numbers! Mum always pushed me to learn my times tables (parrot fashion- who remembers?!) and for that I'm grateful, although I wasn't at the time.

My working career started at 12 selling ice-creams from a trike in town. Mum and dad encouraged me to learn the meaning of money from an early age. I then worked at a country park for a summer and got a job in a farm shop at 14 which I kept for five years. I've always had a strong work ethic, growing up on a farm and seeing how hard mum and dad worked milking cows and chasing them through the fields made an impact. That also helped my maths counting them in and out of the dairy and field!

I studied nursery nursing at college and went onto be the manager of a day nursery taking my baby son with me. When my daughter was born it made no sense financially to take them both to work with me. In the meantime my now ex-husband had bought into a franchise and we decided that I would take on running the accounts department. I trained myself in Sage and learnt about VAT returns, bank reconciliations and ledgers. We successfully ran the franchise and took on another two over the years. I was responsible for the HR and admin as well as the bookkeeping and we employed about 18 staff. I was lucky as I worked school hours and had flexibility to be there for my kids' sports days, assemblies and could drop them off and pick them up from school. We had a nice house, cars, holidays and a boat!

In 2017 my life was rocked when he told me he was leaving me. I was in shock as I hadn't seen it coming. We went through a horrid divorce, I suffered a breakdown and many horrible words were said. This really knocked my confidence - I was 'only data entry' after all. During the divorce it became apparent that my ex-husband would keep the businesses and I would have to find myself a new income stream to pay the bills. I couldn't face being employed after being my own boss for nearly 20 years, even though the kids were older I still wanted flexibility to be with my cockapoo Harley. I want to be around for the kids and do what I want to when I want. I bought into another franchise which was mis-sold to me and sadly I had to escape, losing money, time, and more confidence in the process.

I managed to free myself in June 2020 and I set up Bluebell Admin Services Ltd the following week. I set up a limited company from the beginning as that's what I knew, and I still prefer working with companies as my clients now. Over time the business made me realise that the bookkeeping was what I wanted to focus on, and I think I have manifested that dream.

Finding the 6 Figure Bookkeepers' Club has been an absolute God-send to me and my business. I am currently rebranding to be Bluebell Bookkeeping and Admin as people see me as more of a VA when I'm networking, whereas I want to be known as the go-to bookkeeper in my networks. At first it was so scary but now I love it, I have gained so much confidence.

I am based on the Hants/ Berks/ Surrey border in Hook, Hants but work remotely with clients in Wiltshire, the Isle of Wight and even Scotland! My clients are all VAT registered, Ltd companies and I have a huge variety from retail, builders, gym, consultancies and coaches. I love getting to know the businesses and the business owners and I love it when a client tells me they now love their books or Xero and Sage, as we make it fun, supportive and sustainable by being paperless.

My biggest joy though is my two now young adults, my partner, family and friends witnessing the change in me and telling me how proud they are of me for getting through and continuing to grow and flourish. I know that I can do this and I'm stronger than I realised. I have now done presentations and participated on virtual panels to talk about bookkeeping- something I would never have imagined doing two years ago- thanks 6FB!

My advice to anyone would be to get onto social media, start networking and even apply for jobs. Put the suggestion into the employer's mind of outsourcing instead of employing - they may not have thought of it - my first client hadn't and he's still with me now! Also, find your tribe and get support - I highly recommend the 6FB for that! I love the support between each other and that no question is ever silly. It's definitely 'collaboration over competition' and I have truly made some great friends within the group.

Connect with Claire

www.bluebelladmin.co.uk

Instagram: @bluebelladmin

BOOKKEEPERS' STORIES

Karen Kennedy - Kennedy Accountancy

Above all else, my family motivates me, and I have built my business to enable us to have the life we want. To me, that doesn't mean millions in the bank, it means flexibility, financial freedom and a balance so we get to spend lots of time together doing fun things. The flexibility aspect really drives me - I want to be able to go for a run in the middle of the day if I want, or go to sports day without the guilt that I would have had in my previous jobs. We live in the most beautiful part of the world and being able to get outside and enjoy that is really important to me. Sometimes, the work can wait! And having flexibility means I can pick that up in the evenings if need be.

Previous jobs have really inspired me to build a business which people want to work for, and are treated fairly. And where they are actively encouraged to spend as much time as possible doing things they want to do, whatever that may be, all whilst getting the work done. I've done the working on Christmas Eve and Boxing Day in the past and that will never happen at Kennedy Accountancy. Ever!

I was the FD of a college prior to setting up the business. Whilst it was great experience in certain ways, I never truly believed in it or was inspired by it...too many politics and too much red tape, and too many academics dare I say it! When COVID hit, my husband was still going out to work as a key worker, I had Willie who was four at the time and Archie who was one, both at home with me while I was still working full time trying to keep a college afloat. It was absolutely brutal. I was turning day into night and working nightshifts basically to get the work done - there was no way I could do it during the day with the boys, nor did I want them to remember Covid as me being stuck in front of a computer in meetings all day. They were just too young to be left to themselves. It was during that time it really hit home that I really didn't care enough about my job - yes, I always wanted to do a good job but ultimately just didn't believe in that college's purpose when COVID was happening.

Life is really too short. So, I didn't sit around waiting for some sort of sign or any clients . I just applied for my practice licence, got it then handed in my notice. I had to work a three month notice period, during which time I did some CPD, set up a website with the help of a friend, put an ad in the local paper and then off I went! I had no clients - none. So no, you don't need clients to start. YOU JUST NEED TO START! It was risky leaving a 50k a year job but I knew I could do it. Belief was the only thing I had, but that was all I needed.

Kennedy Accountancy is based in the Scottish Highlands, in a very close knit community. My niche is my local community, and those businesses who are willing to embrace tech.

My biggest challenge is that I'm growing fast with unexpected demand and my proudest moment has been being shortlisted as a finalist at the Accountancy Excellence Awards for New Firm of the Year. Seeing my name in lights in London was just the best!

For anyone thinking of starting their own practice, I'd say just start. Be relentless. Work hard. Know your why. Get into a network of like-minded people doing the same thing - 6FB obviously - you will need support from your peers.

Connect with Karen

kennedyaccountancy.com
Facebook: @Kennedy Accountancy
Instagram: @kennedyaccountancy
LinkedIn: linkedin.com/Karen Kennedy CA

Sarah Kitchener - Olive Branch Bookkeeping Ltd

I'm Sarah. A mum to Sid (aged nine), wife to Matt (age withheld!) and owner of many pets; two cats, one dog, fish and two tortoises. One of our family hobbies is skateboarding. My son is amazing at it; me not so much. During the opening day of our new skatepark, I fell off and broke my wrist before it even officially opened. I'm motivated by a desire to help people make sense of something they don't understand. I also find being a good role model for my son is a great driving force and gives me my 'why'.

I've been working in accounts related roles since I was at college, which is around 15 years ago. I started working in the cash office for my local Argos, which I loved. I moved into my first full-time role as an Accounts Assistant for a finance leasing company. From there, I went on to multiple different accounts roles over the years. Later, I worked for a local publishing company. I started as a finance assistant and worked my way up to Finance Manager. I then joined a company working with software testers as their bookkeeper AKA MoneyBoss (best job title ever) before I set up my own practice.

I set up my practice for a number of reasons. One was my desire to support my family after my husband unexpectedly had a breakdown a few years ago. I also wanted to prove to myself that I am good enough to do it.

I had a difficult time after my parents separated when I was 10. I won't go into detail about the emotional abuse. Ultimately, one thing I was repeatedly told was that I was a disappointment. I studied while raising my son and working full-time. It was a long slog, but I knew it had to be done so that I could set up my own business. It remains one of my proudest achievements. I love helping people go from chaos to calm, so working through people's bookkeeping is my version of mindfulness.

Olive Branch Bookkeeping Ltd is my business name. I love the wordplay on 'reconciliation' by offering an olive branch. I am based in Lewes, East Sussex, surrounded by the beautiful South Downs.

My client niche is those who are independent-led businesses that mainly offer food (another love of mine). I have a range of clients, from those who make stunning customised cookies to others who run coffee shops.

Going at it alone has been the biggest challenge I've faced in business. This was mostly because I didn't really know any other independent bookkeepers until I found the 6 Figure Bookkeepers group. I suffer with self-doubt and I think setting up with no one to talk things through with was really hard. However, it did mean I could set my practice up naturally and exactly how I wanted it.

Running the business alongside various personal issues has been really hard, especially this year. My husband has high functioning ASD, previously called Asperger's. We've been together for 17 years. Although I have been aware he is different; he's only accepted this in recent years. With all the changes that lockdown has enforced upon us all, he has struggled dramatically and it breaks my heart. I want to make my practice a success so he can step back and take the time he needs to find his way again.

My proudest moment in business was having my practice licence approved. I felt like I'd been working so hard with my studies alongside working full time. When the email came through to say it had been approved, I literally broke down. All the emotions hit me at once. I swear my husband thought I was crazy when I opened the door in tears.

Every time a client asks to work with me it still blows my mind. So, I guess I still have little twinges of self-doubt in there. I'm always privileged and humbled when someone trusts you enough to share their financial information with you.

I've come to realise that the most important thing is taking the first step and giving it a go. I knew that even if my practice failed, I would never forgive myself for not trying. There are so many people we can help out there, they just need to find us.

Connect with Sarah

www.olivebranchbookkeeping.co.uk

Facebook & Instagram: @olivebranchbookkeepingltd

Craig Moore - L&M Bookkeeping

My main motivation for becoming a bookkeeper, and more generally, is my 12-year-old daughter. After her mum passed, it was just the two of us. I take a lot of strength from doing things to ensure she grows up into a person her mum would have been proud of.

I started my career in telesales. By a completely bizarre turn of events, I landed up in a credit control role for a major telecoms company. This led me to develop my skills in credit and risk management, working for a number of household name businesses in different sectors. Twenty years later, I decided that I needed to keep the promise that I made myself to leave the corporate world and embark on my self-employment journey.

The passing of my daughter's mum meant that I had to make a lot of life changes. The main one was centred around being there for my daughter more. Working for large organisations meant that

I was always required to put the work of the company first and my personal life second. Developing my own bookkeeping business was the perfect way to enable me to change my priorities.

My business is called L&M Bookkeeping and it's based in Norfolk. We're in a coastal village a few miles outside Great Yarmouth. My main clients are in the construction industry and I spend a lot of my time helping them understand their obligations around CIS and VAT. It wasn't the niche that I had originally picked for myself, but being a bit of a manly man, I think it has ended up being a good fit.

Juggling setting up my business while still being employed full-time and running a house as a single parent has definitely tested my resolve at times. As well as this, it's often been challenging trying to learn all of the practical stuff that your qualifications don't teach you, such as setting up agent codes with HMRC and adding services that you can complete for a client. My sense of achievement when I got the practice licence and took on the first paying client was probably my proudest moment.

My best piece of advice for those starting out would be to just 100% commit and go for it. Life is too short not to follow your dreams; I know this from personal experience.

Connect with Craig

Facebook & Instagram: @landmbookkeeping

Lucy Nichols - LMN Bookkeeping Plus

I am one of four siblings, so family is a big part of my life. I see them almost every weekend. I have two daughters (Millie and Betsy) and four nieces (Violet, Edie, Iris and Annie). At school, I loved maths and always knew I wanted to work with numbers. When I was 14, I was diagnosed with diabetes, which was, and still is, tricky to manage. I also have autism, dyslexia and dyspraxia. In short, I am probably the clumsiest person you will ever meet.

I had my first 'proper' job as a dispenser in a doctor's practice. I left this job shortly before I fell pregnant with my second daughter. From there, I landed my first office job. The director of the company I worked for became my first client when I set up LMN Bookkeeping Plus Ltd.

Since becoming a single parent, I have been determined to be a positive and successful role model for my two girls. In 2015, when Betsy was nearly two, I decided to go back to college to study AAT.

In 2017, I landed my first bookkeeping job in a local accounts practice.

I started LMN Bookkeeping Plus in April 2021. I planned to launch in January, however, home-schooling put this on hold. After trying my hand at it, I soon realised teaching wasn't for me. I then made the decision to go LTD in June 2021 as I felt this was my future. I have a range of clients including construction (limited companies and sole traders), retail (limited and partnerships), rental and many more. Most of my clients are in construction, so this is definitely my niche. I enjoy working in CIS.

My biggest challenge has been confidence. Sometimes I question myself over the silliest things, when in reality I know the answers. The process has shown me that I just need to slow down and believe in myself. Another challenge has been investing time into different software and processes. I would love to get to the position where I need to employ someone, so setting everything up as if I had an employee already has been the most valuable piece of information I've received. This will position me well so that when I get to that stage in my business, it should be a much more fluid transition.

My proudest moment has definitely been taking part in the bookkeepers bootcamp in September, hosted by the amazing Zoe and Jo. I created my business Facebook page and within a week I had a sales call. I secured the client. This gave me the confidence and ambition to carry on and grow my practice even further.

If anyone is thinking of starting their own practice, then my advice would be to just go for it! It can be very daunting at first, but the hard work will pay off. The 6 Figure Bookkeeper group on Facebook has offered an amazing community. I have met some lovely and inspiring people there. It feels like an extra family that I didn't know I had. The Bookkeepers' 6 Month Success Programme is also a great investment that every bookkeeper making the leap to start their own practice should do.

Connect with Lucy

Facebook: @LMNBookkeepingPlus
Instagram: @lmn_bookkeeping_plus

Heather Palmer - Ascot Bookkeeping & Accounting Ltd

Looking back now, my High School closely resembled Waterloo Road. Despite this, I was determined this wasn't going to keep me back from achieving great things in life.

My dad died in his early 40's and I know I let him down with my first choice of job (see below). Now, I know that my dad and my late mum would be super proud of what I have achieved to date. I know they'll also be proud of what I'm going to achieve in the future.

I have always had an entrepreneurial brain. My parents were in haulage and I knew they secretly regretted not starting a haulage business of their own many years ago. I didn't want to repeat their mistakes and lead my life being a "cautious Kevin" (that's what I used to call my parents). If I see an opportunity, I go for it. I find it helpful to set goals in life, both material and personal, to keep me focused and driven. My hobbies include motorsport and vintage cars (I have a 1935 Mercedes), so it's fair to say that I'm a total petrolhead. When I am not enjoying cars, I like to keep fit and go skiing.

After leaving school at 15, my first job was working in a factory cutting room making shirts and blouses for M&S and Next. My dad was understandably not amused with this choice of career. The pull factor for me was the attractive salary and the little brown envelope with cash that you received every Friday!

I then worked in retail for Next before going on to be an events planner in the hotel industry. I transitioned careers into oil and gas with BP - my dad would definitely have approved of this. Around 12 years later, I started my own dancewear manufacturing and retail business. We employed 17 staff. I also bought and ran a wedding dress design company and retail shop. The dancewear business came naturally as I had danced since a young age. Later on, I'd danced professionally for many famous individuals, including Neil Armstrong. I also toured with Prince Edward and Sophie Wessex in Doha, Qatar. I taught dance for over 20 years, effectively my hobby became my business. It was hard work, and after 11 years I was ready to move on to pastures new. When my husband's company insisted we both relocate to the South of England on a permanent basis, it seemed like the perfect moment to start something fresh.

When I moved to Ascot, Berkshire in 2010, I had no friends or job, so I knew I had to make a new life for myself. I did some bookkeeping for my own companies back in Scotland, so was lucky to land a job in the first week at the accounts office of The American School in England (TASIS). I was really inspired and motivated by one of my colleagues, who is still a very close friend. She was studying for her CIMA qualification having completed her ICB & AAT previously. I therefore decided to attend Bracknell College to learn bookkeeping. Doing so also meant that I could get out and meet people. I studied City & Guilds, ICB and then AAT.

I was in my 40's when I embarked on my bookkeeping and accounting journey, so it's never too late to start something new. The professional experience I'd gained made bookkeeping an obvious choice as I had a background in running companies. This had given me a real insight into my clients' businesses from both a bookkeeping and a business owners' point of view. Ultimately, my previous experience was a strength and selling point to clients.

My practice is Ascot Bookkeeping & Accounting Ltd based in Ascot Berkshire. We've been in business since 2014. I avoid pigeonholing myself into a niche as I enjoy the huge variety of clients we work with. Our clients include an ex-England & British Lions rugby player, a conductor, a crisis management company (aviation), a historic motor racing team, coffee kiosks, carpet retailers, a car designer and DJs to name just a few.

I used to feel that the fact I was based at home and didn't have an office held me back. On reflection, I think a lot of this was in my mind. It was always difficult to meet clients for the first discovery chat in coffee shops. Making yourself heard for the first time over the noise of the coffee machines was sometimes a challenge and not always the best of professional introductions. Thankfully, due to COVID, working from home has become the norm and no one asks where my office is. Discovery calls are all done on Zoom with

B
O
O
K
K
E
E
P
E
R
S'

S
T
O
R
I
E
S

no noisy coffee machines to compete with. Working alone can sometimes be a challenge. It can be lonely as I like to bounce ideas off people, so the isolation can be tough.

Joining the 6 Figure Bookkeeper Club has been one of the best things I've ever done. Since joining, the business has gone from strength to strength. I've been shortlisted for a Luca Award with ICB and successfully built a practice, which is growing month on month. For anyone thinking about starting a bookkeeping practice, I'd just tell them to go for it. You can create an incredible work/life balance which has no limits. You also have the power to have as many or as few clients as you wish in order to work the hours you want and when you want. The 6 Figure Bookkeeper Club has been instrumental in giving me a community who I can chat to on a regular basis. Surrounding yourself and networking with like-minded people has been my recipe for my success. Business is challenging there's no doubt about it, but if you surround yourself with the best people, anything is possible.

Connect with Heather

www.ascotbookkeeping.co.uk
Instagram: @ascotaccounting
LinkedIn: linkedin.com/in/ascotbookkeeping
Clubhouse @heatherpalmer

Paula Pinder – Pinder Stonehill

I live in Essex with my fiancé and three kids. I love to work out, meditate, read and travel. I am a very family-orientated person. I love to party and celebrate special occasions, however I also love my home and a night on the sofa with family and a blanket.

When I completed my AAT (2006 – 2008), I always wanted to start my own business. I probably have about 10 new and unique ideas for a business each month. Bookkeeping was the one thing that stuck with me though. Until now, I have never believed I could do it myself. I blamed a lack of experience, and so I got a job and stayed there for just over 11 years. .

I worked in mental health for the NHS for over 10 years doing various admin and secretarial roles. In 2020, I was made redundant from my job. I had also just purchased a house around the same time that COVID swept the nation. Along with many others, I was in lockdown and homeschooling my eight-year-old twins. It was at that point that I remembered my goal from many years before to work for myself. This led me to enquire about reinstating my AAT membership and applying for my practice licence.

I initially set up with the business name of Pin-Point Accountancy. It took me approximately three months to come up with my name and it uses the first three letters (pin) of my surname.

When I first started my business, my clients were my close friends. I felt the most comfortable doing that as I knew any problems would be solved amicably. When I joined the 6 Figure Bookkeeper community, I gradually grew the confidence to take on clients outside of my circle of friends. Now, I have a diverse portfolio of clients ranging from property, e-commerce, coaches and many more.

My ideal clients are working mums/mum-prenuers as this is something that resonates with me. I wear multiple hats (mum, wife, businesswoman...to name a few), and so I'd like to support others that are in a similar position to me.

My biggest challenge has been getting in the way of myself with self-doubt. However, since joining the 6 Figure Bookkeeper programme and along with other mentors, I have connected with a lot of people on the same journey as me. This has been an amazing experience as it has allowed me to remove the self-doubt and reach out to the community if I am trying to second guess or self-sabotage myself.

When I received the email from AAT to confirm my licence had been approved it was one of the proudest moments of my career so far. The hard work had paid off. It meant that I was official and could start working for myself to create the work-life balance I want. This was closely followed by the second proudest moment, which was signing my first client.

I have recently started to work with another bookkeeper forming Pinder Stonehill Accountancy. Working with somebody else allows us both to offer additional services, and allows us to grow our practices more sustainably.

My biggest piece of advice is to get a business mentor, especially one you feel comfortable with. The second bit of advice is: Network! Network! Network! By joining groups with like-minded individuals and those on a similar journey to yours, you can share and learn from each other. It also helped me immensely to find accountability partners to hold each other to account and celebrate each other's success. You only have one life and you need to live it in full and unapologetically.

Connect with Paula

www.pinderstonehill.co.uk

Facebook: @pinderstonehill

Instagram: @pinderstonehill

LinkedIn: www.linkedin.com/in/paula-pinder-0602a0163/

Nicci Rowland – Eco Accounts Ltd

B
O
O
K
K
E
E
P
E
R
S'

S
T
O
R
I
E
S

I have many motives for starting my own business. The biggest one is my children. I want to be able to work around them for convenience, but also so I can be there for them when they need me. The bigger picture is setting an example for them. I want them to grow up to be motivated to work and to know they can do what they love. When they see me following my dreams, they know it's totally possible for them too!

I've always worked in admin since leaving school after my GCSE's. I started a maths and a computing A-level at college, but just before I was due to start, due to family issues, my younger sister, brother and I found ourselves staying with various friends and family, where no one made me go to college. After two weeks, I quit college and found work. Determined to be independent, I did a bit of temping work and ended up working directly for the recruitment agency for six years. Then I was lucky enough to get the chance to live and work in Dubai for 2½ years as a PA, which I absolutely loved! We came back to the UK and I worked in customer service for The Body Shop for two years. Then left for maternity leave and took a career break for seven years to raise the children.

When my firstborn was 18 months old, I started a zoology degree. After the first year, I realised that this career and the travelling for the degree was no longer aligned with the direction I wanted for my life. When baby number two came along, a new dream of finding a career that would work around family life came into focus. I realised I've always enjoyed numbers, maths, finance and being organised so becoming a bookkeeper seemed like an obvious choice. I studied AAT level 2 and 3 at my local college and discovered that I really loved the principles and rules.

When I stumbled on the 6 Figure Bookkeeper's club on Facebook, I very quickly started to dream bigger. Inspired by Jo and Zoe's passion and encouragement, I decided I wanted to run my own successful bookkeeping practice. Everyone in the 6 Figure Bookkeeper community had a role in supporting me to realise my passion of becoming a bookkeeper. All the posts, comments and help were always 100% supportive and positive.

My business is called Eco Accounts Ltd and is based in sunny Bognor Regis. I have decided to niche in the eco-conscious and sustainability markets because I want to help new planet-friendly businesses to grow. By doing this, I feel I am helping them to make a difference. I love being part of the green community too as it inspires me to do better with my environmental goals wherever I can.

BOOKKEEPERS' STORIES

At this early stage, my main challenge is getting clients. I am told that getting the first few clients is the hardest. I am anticipating that once I can demonstrate my skills and get some positive reviews under my belt, there will be a snowball effect. My main short-term goal is to spend time improving my marketing skills, which will help me find the clients I need.

My proudest moment so far was having my first Zoom call as a bookkeeper. I was very nervous, but I know communication will be a big part of my service so I really want to be good at it. It's really important that my clients feel comfortable with me and enjoy talking shop!

There is a lot more of the actual 'business' side of things than I had anticipated. A good supportive group – like the 6 Figure Bookkeeper one – has been instrumental in helping me understand that I am running both a bookkeeping service and a business as well. Once you get started, you may even find you enjoy the' business' side more than the bookkeeping. It can be great fun and liberating to be your own boss.

Connect with Nicci

www.ecoaccounts.co.uk

Instagram: @ecoaccountsltd

Lottie Saunders – Lottie Saunders Bookkeeping

B
O
O
K
K
E
E
P
E
R
S'

S
T
O
R
I
E
S

Before I was a bookkeeper, I was a forensic psychologist working in serious crime with the police on a national level. That just didn't fit in with having a family, so I had a career break and worked in education for a couple of years. Soon after I became a VA and decided that bookkeeping was what I really wanted to do!

I'm really motivated by working with small companies and particularly solopreneurs. I really want to be able to see them succeed in their business and to help them realise their dreams and fly. I particularly like working with soul led businesses and practitioners.

I have been self-employed for a number of years. My children and I have a chronic pain condition with numerous complications and serious side issues. Being self-employed and working on my own schedule means that I can work around these issues, whilst always being able to make medical appointments.

I have been running my practice since February 2021 and I am currently finishing off my Level 4. I'm in the early stages of launching a membership and course as well as writing a journal for my clients to help them achieve their dream business and finances to match. In addition, in September I am starting my qualifications as a Financial Coach specialising in working with women who have suffered a traumatic relationship with money - as part of this I will be doing voluntary work with victims of abuse and also female prisoners - helping them to develop a healthy relationship with money which in turn will help them with their confidence. Finally, I'm also in the process of organising a retreat in Spain with two of my clients - one is a PT and the other is a Sports Masseur and a yoga teacher. I will be involved from the mindset point of view and will also be running business financial drop in sessions as all those involved are running their own businesses.

My business is growing in a really healthy way - I have got rid of a PITA client and now have a multi-million corporate client - which I had never dreamed of having. I have two sub-contractors and am looking to keep growing so that I can help more and more businesses. A real bonus of running your own business is that you can work with people you choose to work with and you can choose your clients - never be afraid to say no if you don't feel someone is a good fit for you. My favourite bonus of working as a remote bookkeeper is that I can work from anywhere - I am off to Spain to work remotely from there for two months every summer.

Connect with Lottie

Lottiesaunders.com

Instagram: @lottiesaundersbookkeeping

Lorna Shakesheff FIAB - LCS Bookkeeping and Payroll Services

I have lived in the same town since I was born. I married my husband, who lived a few doors away from us when I was five. We moved, but ended up in the same street again! We have been together for 26 years and married for 16. We are blessed with two children who are 16 months apart – we like a challenge! Our oldest has ASD, whilst he is a teenager, he still needs personal care and support. My daughter loves to dance and has four classes a week. We all enjoy long dog walks over the local fields, woods and rivers. Pre-COVID, we would regularly go to the cinema or theatre with friends. I have just signed up for a gym membership - at long last, something for me.

Before I was a bookkeeper, I was a PA as I worked through the AAT qualification. I was then fortunate to work for an amazing company in children's travel. I stayed for 13 years as an Accounts

Assistant where I prepared monthly management accounts and reconciled the control accounts.

My son has required lots of support at school over the years. High school was a terrifying thought. There was a chance I would need to do a 32-mile round trip twice a day to attend a school out of town. I also wondered if he would thrive, or if I would be called in for urgent meetings. So, I started my bookkeeping business to give back some control over these things.

My business is currently called LCS Bookkeeping and Payroll Services and we're based in Ledbury. I work directly out of my home. My clients are mainly from the hair and beauty industry. I focus on clients who are starting a new business and help them understand tax, how bookkeeping works, registrations and important dates. I enjoy supporting them with what initially seems very scary.

I started to test the water in 2016, with a plan to leave my job in 2018. An unexpected circumstance made me jump out of employment in 2017. At the same time, I engaged with a large client who required 30 hours a week of bookkeeping.

This client started to get slower at paying me and it was becoming apparent that remote working wasn't suiting the engagement. I handed in my notice and was left with nothing; no clients and limited experience.

I'd say this was one of my biggest challenges, but it was also a learning opportunity for me to upskill and fully commit to my bookkeeping business. I gained software certifications and refreshed my knowledge very quickly, rather than following the initial plan of waiting until 2018. In the end, it was the best thing that could have happened.

My only regret is that I wish I had found the 6 Figure Bookkeepers much earlier. I have learned the hard way from charging too little, not documenting processes, working with non-ideal clients, which resulted in a lot of stress. I'd encourage everyone to do as many of their courses as possible. One of the main takeaway messages for me was to get everything in place first, including the pricing, processes and software.

Despite the challenges of supporting clients through furlough, I was very proud to be the Finalist Bookkeeper of the Year for the IAB in June 2021. I can now say that "I'm at capacity" with ideal clients, which is every business owners dream, right? Developing this business also means that I have created something of a legacy and opportunities for my family, as I might be able to provide my son with employment in a few years.

Connect with Lorna

www.lcsbookkeeping.co.uk
Instagram: @lcsbookkeeping_payroll
LinkedIn: linkedin.com/posts/lorna-shakesheff-fiab

Laura Sterian - LAS Accounting Ltd

I don't want to live in survival mode, where you count every penny to make ends meet. I want to have enough money so that I can help my family, travel and shop without worrying about my bank account balance.

Before I was a bookkeeper, I had two main roles. I was (still am) a certified interpreter and translator. I also worked in academia, but on temporary contracts. So in other words, I was always worried about what I would do when the contract ended.

I became a bookkeeper for two main reasons. Firstly, I wanted to have a profession that can bring money in at any time. I have no interest whatsoever in medical science or in law. I remembered that many years ago, I took a university course in accounting and really enjoyed the work. Based on this, I decided to begin a career change and transitioned into accounting. Secondly, I wanted my own business. I knew that I couldn't work 9 to 5 for an employer. It makes me feel like I am wasting my life for someone else's

BOOKKEEPERS' STORIES

dream and prosperity. Having my own business means that I am independent. I work the hours that I want, whenever I want. I also get to travel whenever I want, which is a massive perk. In other words, I get to be my own boss; I am free and not a slave.

My business name is LAS Accounting Ltd. I am still at the stage where I am preparing the systems of the business. Soon, I will go public to attract potential customers. I am based in Edinburgh, but considering that the business is virtual, I can take clients from anywhere in the UK. As much as I would like to niche, because I understand the reasoning behind it, I have not yet decided what industry to focus on. My ideal client is someone who pays on time, is easy to get along with and does not constantly call with questions. I would take a great client from any background over a challenging one from any particular familiar sector. Once I start onboarding clients, my goal is to find a niche naturally. In an ideal world, I would like to work with libraries and writers.

Some of the biggest challenges I have faced are the practical ones. This has included deciding what software is best for me (i.e. Xero, Sage or Quickbooks). It was also initially difficult to find the funds to invest in starting up the business, with course fees, exam fees, websites and software subscriptions all needing purchasing. Ultimately, I am so glad I did as it means I can now move onto the next step - finding clients!

Connect with Laura

las-accounting.co.uk

LinkedIn: linkedin.com/in/las-accounting-ltd-551171228/

Sarah Twigg - Twigg Accountancy Services

I'm a Licensed Accountant and Bookkeeper with AAT. I'm very family orientated and I love to build communities including ones in crafting and gaming. I thoroughly enjoy helping people and can often be found hanging out in a Facebook group, gaming on stream or walking my dog through the woods.

I was a Management Accountant and had been for four years split between two companies. I'd always worked in industry and never in practice. I was, however, unhappy in my job role. I always had it in my mind to strike out on my own but that was the catalyst - alongside finding the 6 Figure Bookkeeping group and the Startup Programme!

I run Twigg Accountancy Services - Leaf the stress behind ;) !! I decided quite early on that I only wanted to work with medium sized businesses, preferring one to five clients over say twenty five,

BOOKKEEPERS' STORIES

with recurring income and power hours to bolster that income if necessary for the clients. I currently have four clients that are regular weekly/monthly clients - two are from the creative industry, one is from the entertainment industry and one is a fellow bookkeeper!

At the time of writing, my business has been running for just six weeks and managing my time has been a big challenge - with around 40 enquiries in the first six weeks, it's been a bit mad. In future, I need to work out who I *need* to speak to and who I cannot help earlier than the Clarity Call.

I think creating content for social media has been quite tough - initially I thought that would be the easy bit but consistency is key. And it turns out I have an Instagram phobia!!

My proudest moment so far in business has been securing my first client. I was over the moon. That someone trusted me running their accounts department was a BIG confidence boost.

Here's my advice to somebody thinking about starting their own bookkeeping business. Imagine you are 60 now, in this moment. Look back at your life. Do you regret never even giving it a go?

I knew I would. So I decided to jump in, both feet, deep end! And here I am. In a book! On a podcast! With clients in six weeks. Making my "lost" salary back! I didn't think I could do it. I honestly didn't. I probably would've read what I'm writing here about six months ago and thought "Yeah, it's alright for you to do it, but you're not me." And I'm not, you're right.

But I can tell you categorically that if I can do it, then you absolutely can. You've got this!

Connect with Sarah

Facebook: @Twiggaccountancyservices

Facebook: @sarahtwigg123

LinkedIn: linkedin.com/in/sarah-twigg-b85236191

BOOKKEEPERS' STORIES

Mylien Verboom – MCas Accounting & Tax Services

I'm a self-starter and always have been. Many things motivate me, but happiness and good health are the top two. I love being part of a very close-knit family. I have five siblings and we all get on well (most of the time). My children mean the world to me. Outside of bookkeeping/accounting, my hobbies are running and walking.

I have been a corporate accountant for many years, I was trained in the city as a management accountant with a fund management company. I started my accounting and tax practice toward the end of 2020, when my work in the aviation sector slowed down due to COVID. As a practice, I do everything from bookkeeping to tax planning and advice.

We are based in Surrey and London. The practice name is MCas Accounting & Tax Services. As we are still very new to the market, we currently take on all clients. However, we tend to have two prominent streams of clients; landlords/property developers and eCommerce.

Business has lots of challenges in it, so sometimes it's hard to know where to begin! When we first started off the HRMC agent code took nearly two months to sort out. Then, we didn't do our research and got our pricing all wrong. We only quoted for 25% of the market going rate. Customers loved it and we got lots of clients very quickly, but we needed to sort it pretty quickly. We have since realigned some of our clients' fees and are working towards a more standardised approach when onboarding new clients. It's all part of the steep learning curve of starting a business.

We have hit several key milestones which are always a source of great pride with any business. First was the first £5k billing, then achieving our first 20 clients. A little further down the line we achieved 5-digit billing within six months.

My best piece of advice for anyone is to ask, "what are you waiting for?" Do it! It's the most rewarding thing, but also a lot of hard work. Being your own boss means that you will appreciate your own hard work! I enjoy the freedom and that flexibility of working hours to fit around my family.

Connect with Mylien

www.mcas.co.uk

Facebook: @MCasAccounting

Instagram: @mcasaccountingandtax

Kath Vincent - Long White Cloud Accounting

I love numbers and helping people. I get a great sense of achievement when I can use my accounting knowledge and expertise to make other business owners' lives easier and more straightforward. I also love doing prescriptive hobbies like following some music to play or a knitting or cross stitch pattern to follow. Exercise classes where I need to keep up with the beat are a fav.

I've been working in the accounting world for twenty years. I've had many accounting jobs across all types of sectors, mainly working in the Management Accounting departments of NHS hospitals and I started my own practice to give me the flexibility and ability to work from home.

When lockdown hit, I was forced to work from home, it was great! I had two part time jobs. One was always at home, the other involved three short school hours days, two in the office and one at home.

I decided to give up my stressful final ACCA exams as I'd had a stint working in a chartered accountancy firm but did not like it one bit and took stock of why I needed ACCA (I didn't).

So with some extra time to fill I started looking for a third part time job and came across the 6 Figure Bookkeepers' Club on Facebook. I could not believe that without being a Chartered Accountant I was able to become an AAT Licensed Accountant and set up my own business. Setting up my own business after getting my AAT practice licence has been one of my proudest moments, I was not even aware that there was such an avenue possible for me. My mum always thought that when I had kids, starting my own business would be a great idea. I had always said "it's not possible because I don't have the right qualifications and experience".

She is always right.

My business is called Long White Cloud Accounting. I grew up in New Zealand and Aotearoa is the Maori name for New Zealand, meaning The Land of the Long White Cloud. I'm based near Sutton, near London and I niche in working with local, progressive, digital minded VAT registered limited companies. My current clients include a food led hospitality company and a global telecommunications software provider.

I've faced the typical challenges of a new practice owner since starting up in 2021. I needed the confidence to take the leap to start up, then I had to address my pricing, and I needed to get a clear message out there about what I can do for small businesses. I have accounting in my name and I am an accountant but what I really want to do is bookkeeping. When I started my business, I didn't understand the general business population's needs and pain points. I have a long way to go in getting my marketing clear and targeted and I think in general, the bookkeeping world also has a long way to go in convincing the world of business that bookkeepers are where it's at. We are the grass roots of your business finances, we work with you throughout the year and help you plan for growth. We are not just data entry, low paid business noobs!

For anyone thinking of starting a bookkeeping practice, take a look at The 6 Figure Bookkeepers' Club and take the six week Bookkeepers' Startup Programme. Before doing this, I was totally overwhelmed and all over the show, I think it would have taken a year to get started properly without doing this programme.

It's a lot of hard work to start your own practice and you have to persevere but it's totally worth it. Make sure you start out with a really clear why. Why are you starting on this challenging journey of setting up your own business? Write it down where you can see it and keep coming back to it.

Connect with Kath

www.longwhitecloud.co.uk
Facebook & Instagram: @lwcaccounting
linkedin.com/in/kathryn-vincent

Libby Walklett - The Ethical Bookkeeper

I'm motivated by my family and friends. I want to be able to spend more time with them, and to have time for my hobbies. I try hard to focus on having a balanced life (something I'm not great at!). I'm also motivated by being able to help other people with their finances - whether that's personal or business finance. I get a big kick out of supporting others.

I started working in a newsagents at 14. At 16 I went to work part time for a restaurant chain. I was quickly asked to work full time, before being moved around the country and promoted to Supervisor and, later, to Deputy Manager, managing a hotel as well as a very busy restaurant. After six years, I needed a better balance and left to pursue an admin role, (with a few bookkeeping duties thrown in) for a company selling industrial lawnmower parts. I halved my salary overnight, and I had a mortgage to pay, but it was absolutely worth it! Over the next few years I moved from company to company and took on roles where I was able to learn sales ledger, credit control, purchase ledger, payroll, foreign expenses and more, until I took up a senior role working for a Leisure Group, producing four weekly management accounts for seven limited companies, and payroll at the same frequency, meeting with auditors and directors regularly. I was specifically taken on to cover the group accountant, and had only three months to fully understand the role. That was an incredibly steep learning curve but, with much determination, and quite a few hours of unpaid overtime, I managed the role successfully, and stayed with them for seven years until I was forced to leave due to moving half way across the country.

I have, in various roles, felt undervalued and have struggled to find real job satisfaction and hours to suit being a mum. I was also fed up with working for and with people who could be unreasonable, unethical, unsupportive and unappreciative. I wanted to prove I could do it; prove I could run a successful business and offer the sort of exceptional service that I would want as a customer. Too often, business owners over-promise and under-deliver. I don't want to be that sort of person!

My business was rebranded in 2021 and is now The Ethical Bookkeeper. This has led to a number of interesting conversations about what ethical means to me. Well, I am trying to run a sustainable practice - reduce energy, paper, printer ink, use ethical suppliers, but also work with clients that are ethical too. I want to adhere to best practice - paying suppliers to term or earlier. Then there's the service I want to offer - I adhere to the AAT Code of Ethics - I would never pretend to be an expert or offer advice without ensuring I really know what I'm talking about. I treat my clients the way I like to be treated - and the same goes for their suppliers and customers if I have to deal with them direct. I also chose the name to avoid taking on the sort of client that wants to claim for everything, but doesn't want to produce receipts.

I think, as time passes, the challenges change. Sometimes, things that can appear insurmountable, actually aren't that bad once you tackle them. The challenge is in your thoughts more than the reality. At the time of writing, my biggest challenge is finding the right time to leave paid employment - I'm not a big risk taker, and I don't want to let my family down by not bringing in enough money to support them. Then, keeping up with changes in legislation and technology when you're a sole trader can by immense - I don't think people always realise just how tough it can be to set up on your own. I knew it was going to be hard, but even then, I underestimated how much there was to do. The changes in software have been immense over the last couple of years and I have suffered from overwhelm - I think that's very common. That's why it's so important to have a support network in place when you set up.

There have been many small moments that made me feel proud. Seeing my new logo; receiving my bookkeeping licence and, more recently, my accounting licence; supporting my clients with speedy, high quality service. Those moments when you sort out a longstanding issue for your client painlessly and they think you are the best thing since sliced bread!

My advice to somebody thinking of starting their own business is to find your tribe. Working for yourself is daunting, scary, isolating.

B
O
O
K
K
E
E
P
E
R
S'

S
T
O
R
I
E
S

Having the support of your family and friends is wonderful. Having a network of other self employed bookkeepers and accountants is the most amazing, incredible gift you can give yourself.

Connect with Libby

www.theethicalbookkeeper.co.uk

Facebook: @EthicalBK

Instagram: @theethicalbookkeeper

Twitter: @EthicalBK

LinkedIn: linkedin.com/in/financial-controller-libby-walklett-91954a98/

Jana Ward - Brush Up Accounting Ltd

I'm the founder of Brush Up Accounting Ltd, and am passionate about helping women to understand their finances, growing their business, and being financially independent, because I was once a single parent who struggled with working full time and studying for my AAT qualification at the same time.

I grew up with my parents building their business. My mum is an accountant, so there was never much of a question about what was I going do. I finished my Diploma in accounting in the Czech Republic then came over to England to do a bit of travelling. While in England, I have worked in lots of different roles. Initially, I worked as a barista whilst learning English (my coffees were about as good as my English was). I also worked as a secretary for a big recruitment company in London. It was enjoyable, but I always knew I could do a lot more than I was doing.

I had my daughter when I was 28 and my son a couple of years later. My children are my biggest motivation. I want to be there for them and provide a good life for them. My goal has been to teach them that they can achieve anything they choose to, just like my parents taught me, and to be who they want to be, not who they are expected to be.

After having the children, we moved from London to Telford. It was very different to London and there weren't many flexible jobs. I started working as a carer in the evenings and weekends so that I could spend time with my children during the day. I really enjoyed the job, but the care companies didn't treat their workers well, so I knew it wasn't sustainable.

I became a single mum when my kids were four and six and had to get a full-time job and worked at the local hospital in a Preoperative Assessment department. As it was 9-5 during the week, it gave me time to study AAT in the evening. After moving between lots of different jobs, I wanted something that was more concrete and could provide for my children. I loved completing levels 2 and 3, and I had them done within 12 months. I started to work in accounts for a care company. Later, I moved to an accounts department in a local factory, whilst studying for level 4. I finished it just as COVID-19 began, so it seemed like the perfect timing to set up on my own.

The main reason I started my own accounting practice was my children. I barely saw them whilst working full-time, so I missed out on many life events and being there to support them when they needed me. Working in the factory meant that I left early and came home late. I also missed school events and couldn't stay with them while they were sick. I wanted to change for the sake of my family.

I strive to find the path of least resistance when it comes to getting where I want to be. It's important to be tactical and smart with your time, rather than waste it on unnecessary battles or misguided steps to achieving your goals. I am quite eco-orientated, which lends itself well to a digital business as I don't see a reason to print things out and most things can be done from home – saving unnecessary cost and environmental impact from travelling. My role is to help people get organised painlessly.

One of the biggest hurdles in setting up the company has been understanding how to run my own business. I have worked in other businesses and completed my studies, but neither quite prepared me for every aspect of running my own business.

The 6 Figure Bookkeeper has been great in overcoming these challenges. I would have never been able to set up my practice with such smooth processes and so quickly without trial-and-error process. Being able to speak to Jo, Zoe and all the other bookkeepers has been really valuable in making a range of decisions, especially when it comes to choosing the right software. I'd encourage anyone to join as the course is worth every penny, it will set you on the path of success.

Connect with Jana

www.brushupaccounting.co.uk
Facebook: @jana.ward.58
Instagram: @brushupaccounting
LinkedIn: linkedin.com/in/jana-ward-831b81131/

B
O
O
K
K
E
E
P
E
R
S'

S
T
O
R
I
E
S

Zoe Whitman - The 6 Figure Bookkeeper

In 2016, I said goodbye to my colleagues as I headed off for the Christmas holidays. I was 33 weeks pregnant but knew I would be back for a fortnight in the new year to help with the first 10 working days of the year end. This was really important for my team, we had huge checklists of tasks to complete by the tenth day, these two weeks were always the worst of the quarter, let alone at the year end.

I had a comfortable salary, great colleagues and a job I'd been desperate for a few years previously. The job, however, was very stressful and required long hours, I was exhausted, emotional and overwhelmed. I didn't feel connected to what I did, I didn't feel I made a difference and it's fair to say that I was probably at my emotional limit.

My waters broke the day after Boxing Day and my daughter was born before the new year. Fortunately she was healthy considering her early arrival but I was in shock and it took a while for me to get into motherhood.

I didn't know what to do with myself on maternity leave. I had no interest in baby groups yet to fill the time I dragged my daughter all over the city. We went to baby signing, baby sensory, breastfeeding groups, a baby language group, you name it, we went there. Looking back, it's clear that I needed something to do. Fortunately at the same time, people in my husband's network kept asking if I could help with their tax returns. As a result, I took the necessary training to earn my bookkeeping licence and gain some clients before I went back to work in 2018.

I returned to financial services part-time and managed my clients in the evenings and the half-day per week I had additional child care for. Marketing became a bit of a hobby, I was good at networking and raising my profile, I said yes to every opportunity, I got referrals and I soon found myself taking sales calls in the evenings, weekends and lunch breaks.

One Sunday, I took a call from a client while my daughter had a nap in the park. Afterwards, my husband asked me how much money I was earning. I remember telling him I'd turned over nearly £2,000 so far that month and he suggested I chose to focus on one thing. So, I took a deep breath and decided to leave my job.

The flexibility that came with self employment was enticing, this could be perfect with a young family but my money mindset was

BOOKKEEPERS' STORIES

a huge challenge. I've had the drive to create my own financial stability and security from a young age and my belief was that this only came from a steady job. My mum brought my sister and me up on her own. She's struggled with her mental health for many years so at times my sister and I were looked after by foster carers. Things didn't always feel very stable. I was the sensible, studious type and I felt a deep need to take responsibility for my sister and my mum.

I was good at school. I did well in exams and went to university to study accountancy. Unfortunately, I had to move out of home a few months into my degree. I was desperate to get that degree, to me it was the stamp of approval that I'd "made something of myself", but I dropped out and got a job as a trainee accountant instead. I still remember sitting in the job interview wondering where it had all gone wrong, but I was determined that I was going to be in control of the roof over my head and if that meant parking my degree for a while, so be it. I had a fantastic introduction to accountancy, I got a lot of support from my colleagues and I qualified as an accountant with the ACCA aged 23. I also received my degree six months later thanks to the ACCA's partnership with Oxford Brookes University - something which still runs today and which I highly recommend to every ACCA member.

I've since worked in all sorts of organisations in various finance roles where I've learnt so much. What we do as accountants and bookkeepers is so valuable to those who don't speak our language and I knew that, but having always been an employee, I didn't know how to ensure self employment would bring that same security as my job. I had to work hard on my self belief so I worked with a coach, and as I found the courage, I left financial services to make the bookkeeping business a reality.

A lot happened quickly. I joined a group coaching programme, I found more clients and as the business grew, I took on staff and found an office. We won some awards and I wrote a book. At the beginning of 2020, I also met Jo Wood.

The pandemic wasn't kind and hit my revenue hard and immediately. I'd just started to put my second baby (not quite a 1-year-old at that point) into nursery. The business was set up to run with minimal input from me but marketing and sales weren't systemised, relying upon me heavily. I'd taken my foot off of the marketing pedal for months. I couldn't furlough myself, yet I couldn't work in the business with two preschoolers at home. I did what I knew best as an accountant and ran a cash flow forecast. With a significant dent in our income, no certainty about how long this would last for and no interest in taking out a loan, I made the decision to close up, or at least to park the business while I worked out what to do next.

I count myself incredibly fortunate to have a wonderful and supportive husband. We got through that difficult and emotional time. My social media presence meant I quickly found a job and I was employed for a while but when the opportunity arose, I left to focus all my energy on The 6 Figure Bookkeeper.

Every day I get to help bookkeepers and accountants see the value in what they do. I know how essential it is to have strategy, I love sharing my passion for business and marketing, and listening. Listening to our community is such an important part of what I do because, as I've demonstrated, Jo and I don't know everything. We do have, however, an incredible resource in the network we've been able to grow in the past few years, and I love that we can bring conversations to the bookkeeping world about mindset, strategy and goal setting to wrap around the more practical aspects of building a business.

I love the freedom and flexibility that comes when you run your own business and I want to empower more people to choose work which is right for them. Don't let a story or belief you carry stop you from making an amazing future happen for yourself, be guided by your values instead. Know that your past experiences might create stories with the potential to hold you back, but then use those stories as fuel to build something wonderful for your future. Of course there will be challenges along the way, and things might not turn out as you expect, but you'll learn so much more about business from taking action than you could ever read in a business book.

Contact Zoe

www.6figurebookkeeper.com
Instagram: @_zoewhitman
LinkedIn: LinkedIn.com/in/zoewhitman

Jo Wood - Jo Wood Virtual FD and The 6 Figure Bookkeeper

BOOKKEEPERS' STORIES

When I was one of the first girls at school to pass my driving test, I noticed that there was something different about the way I approached things in life. Lots of the girls were talking about having driving lessons and getting a car one day, but when I drove into the Sixth Form car park in my white Ford Fiesta, I realised I was the kind of person who could make things happen. I'd decided what I wanted, put a plan in place, and achieved my goals.

I've always been business minded. When I was very young, my parents and I lived in and ran a pub, we also had a trophy engraving business. My mum's family were entrepreneurs, my dad had a thirst to be a self-made millionaire and was always hunting out the next deal. I have always taken for granted the full immersion I received into entrepreneurship at such a young age. I didn't know it at the time, but these experiences helped to shape my approach to life and my future success.

As the eldest of five siblings, earning my own money from a young age gave me freedom. It gave me space from my brothers and sisters and the means to buy my own bus fares, makeup and clothes. By the age of just 17, I'd become known as the best village babysitter, while I juggled part time jobs around my school work.

That summer, my boyfriend of 18 months dumped me. I was upset, shocked and angry. But with no issues with self-confidence, I decided I deserved better. I'm a big believer in the Law of Attraction, and I believe that putting out the message to the universe that I was worth more is the reason the man of my dreams walked through my front door two weeks later.

I started my career in retail. I quickly progressed from my shop assistant role at Miss Selfridges to running the shop alone on a Sunday at the age of 18. I was opening the shop, cashing up, managing staff and closing at the end of the day. I loved the responsibility, but I knew I needed more. I joined an accountant's office which was very different from the shop floor of Miss Selfridges. It was so quiet and a bit stale, but I was so excited, and I felt like a grown up. The fact I'd have to go out to clients really thrilled me and the opportunity to have a real career made me work hard in this position. I worked 9 until 5:30 during the week, and then on Saturday and Sunday I would go to London to go to college, where I would learn how to be an accountant. It was extremely full-on and I was being paid less than what I got as a shop assistant, but I knew that was a sacrifice I needed to take in order to gain a respected career.

Over the next few years, I moved to a couple of accountancy firms one in London and then back to a local one in Kent. Here I became an audit senior, this meant I was tasked with going on site to larger companies and auditing their books and records. I spent my days scrutinising their numbers and doing a bit of detective work. I got to spend a lot of time in different businesses. I was with the staff and looking at how these different businesses ran, sometimes I was at these businesses for such a long time that I became part of the team. I was even invited to hen parties and other staff outings. This position gave me a real insight as to how a successful business should be run. I learned the tools to review figures, I used KPIs and learnt to spot areas of concern quickly. I would sit and talk through my findings with the business owner or the finance director. Looking back, this must have been scary at my young age of 20, but it was my job so I didn't think twice about it.

I gained a lot of confidence in those years, I was good at my job, I was passing all of my exams and my superiors were happy with my work. I married my husband Paul in 2002 and I fell pregnant with our first child very quickly. At the age of 22, I became a mum to Daniel. This was mega scary; I had to look after a human being and oversee his every need. I was filled with dread, but I knew I wanted to be at his beck and call and no longer at my employer's. I decided very quickly that I didn't want to return to work so I needed to become self-employed. This didn't scare me that much because I've been brought up in a family full of self-employed people, so it was just what I needed to do. I knew that I couldn't set up as an accountant because I was only part-qualified, but I thought that I could be a bookkeeper. In fact, I thought it would be easy to do.

I took a Sage course with my Mother In Law, Carol, over the weekends and was introduced through my tutor to an accountant who needed some bookkeeping support. Carol would come over and hold Daniel and we would set up an ironing board to place all the paperwork on. It was a great introduction into the world of bookkeeping and it worked so well around my new baby. Unfortunately, I didn't really know what I was doing. I understood largely the end product I wanted to achieve, but with no specific bookkeeping and tax training, I started to make mistakes. So much so that I got the sack!!

For the next two years, I worked as a part-time bookkeeper for a small advertising company. My confidence increased, and when baby number two, Grace was born, I started Aqua Bookkeeping.

My little 14-year-old sister Marie wanted some work experience and to earn some money, so she would come and organise receipts into date order, and help with filing. With her help and Carol's help, we had a proper little business running and we took on more and more clients.

As I grew Aqua Bookkeeping, I decided to take personal development more seriously. I read mindset books, listened to tapes and attended a Tony Robbins event which changed my life. I decided to grow the business with the help of a client who wanted to invest in my business. I took on premises, I took on more staff, more clients and became a limited company.I had all the drive and belief, but I had absolutely no idea how to be a business owner. The business failed fast and although heart broken, I learnt an important lesson in how not to start and run a business.

Over the next few years, I went back to working from home. I was busy looking after two small children and my business grew slowly, but it was manageable. Paul had been working for the government since just before Daniel was born, he thought he had a job for life. Unfortunately, in 2010, we had two big surprises. Paul was made redundant that year just around the time we found out that baby number three was going to make an appearance.

Rosie was born in August 2010 and by the time she was born, we had already decided that I was going to be the one that did the full time work. It made more sense for Paul to be at home with the children than to retrain, so three days after having Rosie, sitting on multiple soft cushions and using a breastfeeding pillow as a laptop stand, I finalised VAT returns and got to work. I had a fire in my belly, my little family needed me and I was going to keep a roof over our heads at all costs. I attended networking meetings, I told everyone that I was looking for new clients, I asked my current clients to tell their friends about me and it worked. I gained lots of new clients, I was really busy and I took the leap to take on new premises again.

I was approached by an accountancy practice who were impressed by what I was doing, and in 2012 I went into partnership with them to head up a bookkeeping and payroll branch. This meant I had warm leads from the accountants coming in a steady stream, so many that I needed staff quickly. Paul and his mum Carol trained in payroll and took over this department and I headed up the bookkeeping side with the help of my two sisters.

The Managing Partner of the accountancy practice took me under his wing and imparted lots of knowledge to me about how to run a profitable practice and how to manage clients. I also worked with a business coach, and studied to gain my AAT Level 4 in this time.

Looking back, I can see why what happened next happened.

I was building a business, a mum of three small children and studying and I was completing exams. I was exhausted and I got ill. I had three operations between October 2013 and March 2014 which left me feeling awful., I had put my body through so much stress that something had to give.

I didn't know what I was going to do, so being the entrepreneur I am, I decided to start a network marketing business with a health and wellness company. My life had to change but we still needed me to earn, so I sold my share of the business and worked on my new venture with the belief it would give me the work-life balance I needed. I worked my socks off, progressed quickly and became a sponge at every seminar and meeting I attended, but in truth I was simply a slave to the network marketing business! I worked so hard and put so much pressure on myself to achieve that I slipped a disc in my back and had to have major spinal surgery in 2015.

I went back to bookkeeping and was quickly snapped up to become the employed finance manager of a would-be-client. When I joined, the business wasn't profitable, and within two years I helped them get to £1m net profit before they surprisingly made me redundant.

In April 2019 I found myself unemployed and starting from scratch, again. This time though, things felt different. . While I had been working 9-5pm Monday to Friday, I found I had time to work on myself, a luxury I'd never given myself before and during that time, I'd invested in a coach who had taught me how to set up an online business.

I knew that I had to replace my income very quickly and I knew that I could set up a bookkeeping practice quickly (5th time lucky!) So I went to work starting Jo Wood Virtual FD.

I used my know-how to start an online business to try new marketing methods to get my name out there. I spoke to everyone I knew and told them the type of businesses I wanted to help and how I could help them. Even though I needed to grow quickly, I was going to be very strict on which clients I took on and decided I would interview them in the discovery call, just as much as they were interviewing me. I only wanted to work with lovely people who would respect my expertise and value my time, Oh and also be my Facebook friend.

From day one I took on a subcontractor. I knew that if I tried to do all the bookkeeping work I couldn't do the marketing, sales, discovery calls, software implementation and management accounts meetings too. So I took on a bookkeeper and Paul, my husband looked after my clients payrolls. I found an accountant to outsource the compliance work to and from here we have steadily built the team to a team of 12 in April 2022 This I'm so proud to say includes our son, Daniel as our apprentice (remember he was the reason I became self-employed in the first place!)

Our focus is very much on the needs and goals of our clients. I have found a niche in salon owners and online business coaches and I can honestly say I never have that horrible feeling when the phone rings or I look at my calendar and see my upcoming appointments. I see my clients as friends and we are in this together. My team is there to support their business and we really focus on communication and keeping things simple.

We are heavily systemised so other team members can take on workload to allow time for illness, holidays or training. We are 100% virtual and digital. We all work from home and never visit a client onsite. I was able to replace my income from my employment within the first ten months and I registered for VAT within 16 months of starting my practice.

I always say that this practice is my final practice, and I'm proud to be able to share what we do at Jo Wood Virtual FD with other bookkeepers because it matters to me so much that you too can make a business which works for you around your health, around your family, and which is successful.

Contact Jo

www.jo-wood.com
Facebook: @JoWoodVirtualFD/
Instagram: @jowoodd
LinkedIn: www.linkedin.com/in/jowood1

Glossary

AAT	Association of Accounting Technicians
Website	aat.org.uk
ACCA	The Association of Chartered Certified Accountants
Website	accaglobal.com
IAB	International Association of Book-keepers
Website	iab.org.uk
ICB	The Institute of Certified Bookkeepers
Website	bookkeepers.org.uk
ICAEW	Institute of Chartered Accountants in England and Wales
Website	icaew.com
CIMA	The Chartered Institute of Management Accountants
Website	cimaglobal.com
KPI	Key Performance Indicator
PITA client	Pain In The Arse client

Acknowledgements

None of this would have been possible without the support of our families giving us the space to have Zoom calls on Saturday mornings during lockdown. Our husbands have happily supported us as we've travelled around the country to make sure we can show up, be present and support our community.

Thank you to the people who've seen the need for this community and stepped in to support us even when nobody was listening yet. Special thanks to Senta by Iris, Ashley Leeds, James Ashford, Pete Scott, the whole team at AccountingWEB, Shirley Mansfield, Dan Cockerton, Caroline Hobden, Carl Reader, the team at FreeAgent, Suzanne Dibble, Abi Rogers, Michelle and Christian Ewen, Andrew and Pete and Zoe Lacey-Cooper and huge thanks to Ben Smith for telling us we should start a podcast, and to Trent Mclaren for being our very first guest.

Thank you to the members of our success lounge for believing in us to support you on this journey of reaching the next stage in your business. You throw yourselves head first into life every day and we love seeing you making money, winning clients, bringing your partners into your businesses, achieving flexibility around childcare, growing teams, collaborating, sharing the highs and the lows, posting on social media, building a personal brand, going live in the Facebook group and achieving your goals. You are pushing yourselves out of your comfort zones and owning your space as the future leaders and influencers of this industry.

Thank you also to 8,000 (and counting) members of The 6 Figure Bookkeepers' Club, you're next.

About the Authors

Jo Wood and Zoe Whitman are both award winning business women within their field. They coach and mentor bookkeepers, accountants and small business owners, and host The Bookkeepers' Podcast.

Jo lives in Kent with her husband, three children, dog and cat. Zoe lives in Monmouthshire with her husband, two children and cats - she's yet to get her dream Springer Spaniel.

Jo and Zoe met at an event in 2019 where they were both speaking. Despite living at different ends of the country, their passion for supporting the bookkeeping community resulted in them founding The 6 Figure Bookkeeper in early 2020.

Jo and Zoe support bookkeepers to start and scale their bookkeeping practices and take their place alongside accountants. They ensure bookkeepers who need support and accountability to go out on their own, are able to charge their worth and build businesses which work for them. You can hear from Jo and Zoe every week on The Bookkeepers' Podcast, you can join them in their free Facebook group the 6 Figure Bookkeepers' Club and you can work with them on their Bookkeepers' 6 Month Success Programme or join them in their Bookkeepers' Success Lounge membership.

Join The 6 Figure Bookkeepers' Club
at 6figurebookkeeper.club

Scan me for FREE TRAINING

6figurebookkeeper.club